HAL LEONARD KEYBOARD STYLE SERIES

R&B KEYBOARD

THE COMPLETE GUIDE WITH CD!

BY MARK HARRISON

Additional music examples by Warren Wiegratz

ISBN 0-634-04660-8

HAL•LEONARD®
CORPORATION

7777 W. BLUEMOUND RD. P.O. BOX 13819 MILWAUKEE, WI 53213

In Australia Contact:
Hal Leonard Australia Pty. Ltd.
22 Taunton Drive P.O. Box 5130
Cheltenham East, 3192 Victoria, Australia
Email: ausadmin@halleonard.com

Visit Hal Leonard Online at **www.halleonard.com**

INTRODUCTION

Welcome to *R&B Keyboard*. If you're interested in playing classic and contemporary R&B styles, but were never quite sure how, then you've come to the right place! Whatever your playing level, this book will help you sound more authentic in your R&B stylings.

After reviewing some essential chords and scales, we'll dig into the voicing techniques and rhythmic patterns that are vital for the R&B keyboardist. We'll focus on "comping" (accompaniment) styles using a variety of keyboard instruments; acoustic piano, electric piano, organ, clavinet, and analog synthesizers. This will help you to create your own keyboard parts on a variety of R&B tunes and progressions!

Seven complete tunes in various R&B styles are included in the "Style File" chapter at the end of the book. Several of these examples also include transcribed keyboard solos. Jam with the rhythm section on these tunes using the play-along CD – this is a great way to develop your keyboard chops within these different rhythmic grooves.

Good luck with your R&B Keyboard!

—*Mark Harrison*

About the CD

On the accompanying CD, you'll find demonstrations of most of the music examples in the book. The solo piano tracks feature the left-hand piano part on the left channel, and the right-hand piano part on the right channel, for easy "hands separate" practice. The full band tracks feature the rhythm section on the left channel, and the piano on the right channel, so that you can play along with the band. Please see the individual chapters for specific information on the CD tracks and how to use them.

About the Author

Mark Harrison is a *Keyboard Magazine* columnist and an educational author whose books are used by thousands of musicians worldwide. His TV credits include *Saturday Night Live, American Justice, Celebrity Profiles,* and many other shows and commercials. As a working keyboardist in the Los Angeles area, Mark performs regularly with the top-flight Steely Dan tribute band Doctor Wu, as well as the critically-acclaimed Mark Harrison Quintet. He has also shared the stage with top musicians such as John Molo (Bruce Hornsby band) and Jimmy Haslip (Yellowjackets), and is currently co-writing an R&B/pop project with the GRAMMY®-winning songwriter Ron Dunbar. For further information on Mark's musical activities and education products, please visit *www.harrisonmusic.com.*

CONTENTS

Chapter 1

WHAT IS RHYTHM & BLUES?

Rhythm and Blues (or "R&B") is an American music style which emerged in the 1950s, and has flourished and developed up until the present day. R&B originally evolved from the jump blues styles made popular in the 1940s, incorporating pile-driving rhythms and vocals tailored to teenage and pop audiences. This new style placed greater emphasis on songs, and had a leaner and less "jazzy" instrumentation. R&B was also an important precursor of the rock 'n' roll styles that emerged in the mid-1950s.

Nowadays the term R&B has come to encompass all "black popular music," and therefore includes various sub-categories such as soul, funk, disco, dance-pop, hip-hop, neo-soul, and so on. In tracing the overall development of R&B from its origins until the present, we will take a brief look at each of these styles and some of their important artists. In Chapters 4 and 5, we will see how to apply these styles to the keyboard.

Early R&B (1950s)

Jerry Wexler at Atlantic Records is credited with shaping the early R&B sound of artists such as LaVern Baker, Ruth Brown, and The Drifters, and with coining the term "rhythm and blues." R&B music from this period also incorporated "doo-wop" groups with intricate and stylized vocal harmonies, such as Vernon Green and the Medallions. Doo-wop remained an influence in R&B styles to come, notably including the "Philly Soul" sound of the 1970s. Also, several 1950s R&B performers began adding gospel and church music influences, such as Ray Charles, Jackie Wilson, and Clyde McPhatter. As well as being a unique vocal stylist, Ray Charles was also an innovative keyboardist who influenced generations of players across the spectrum of blues, soul, and R&B.

This gospel-tinged R&B gave birth to soul music in the 1960s. Soul is arguably R&B's most important offshoot, incorporating R&B, gospel, and pop elements to create a funkier and looser sound. Some important regional soul styles to emerge were Motown soul, Memphis soul, and Philly soul.

Motown Soul (1960s)

The most famous style of soul music originated from Motown Records in Detroit. Motown recordings were characterized by their crisp pop-oriented production, melodic hooks, rhythmic basslines, and strong vocals. Artists such as Marvin Gaye, Smokey Robinson, the Temptations, the Four Tops, the Supremes, Stevie Wonder, and many others, recorded a huge body of work which endures to this day. Motown was the most successful independent label of its era, equally popular with black and white audiences, enjoying huge crossover success on the pop charts.

Memphis Soul (1960s)

The Stax/Volt label in Memphis (absorbed into Atlantic Records in the late 1960s) was the other most notable source of soul music during this period. Theirs was a funkier type of soul, with less polished vocal production and more horn riffs. The house band for most of their recordings was Booker T. and the MG's, and their roster of soul stars included Wilson Pickett, Sam and Dave, Otis Redding, and Carla Thomas.

Philly Soul (1970s)

The "Philly soul" sound was developed by producers Kenneth Gamble and Leon Huff in Philadelphia. This was a highly-produced sound which emphasized string arrangements and doo-wop-style vocal harmonies. Many of their songs also had a gospel influence and some social and political commentary in the lyrics. Noted Philly Soul artists include the O'Jays, Harold Melvin and the Blue Notes, the Three Degrees, and the Intruders.

Other R&B sub-styles which developed from the 1970s onwards, include funk and disco.

Funk (1970s)

In the 1970s, funk emerged as the most rhythmic and earthy variant of R&B. It has been hugely influential on all subsequent R&B styles, as well as on hip-hop and modern/alternative rock styles. This style has a big emphasis on groove and syncopation, often building on the rhythmic foundation of the bass and drums with staccato rhythmic guitar parts. Keyboards also began to take a prominent role, with the percussive clavinet stylings of artists such as Stevie Wonder and Max Middleton. Funk artists were also influenced by the psychedelic and guitar-based rock of the time. Some important artists from this period include James Brown, George Clinton, Parliament/Funkadelic, Bootsy Collins, and Rick James.

Disco (1970s)

Disco emerged as a less soulful, more rhythmically straightforward genre in the mid-1970s. It was specifically a dance music style, emphasizing repetitive basslines and hi-hat patterns. Funk continued to exert a rhythmic influence on disco recordings, typically in a more diluted form. Keyboard players were often called upon to play synth comping parts, as well as piano. Important disco artists include Donna Summer, the Bee Gees, Chic, Sister Sledge, Barry White, and Irene Cara.

All of the R&B sub-styles from the 1980s onwards can be grouped under the "urban contemporary" umbrella (a term first coined by the New York disc jockey Frankie Crocker). These styles are different from pre-1980s R&B in that they use modern production techniques (synthesizers, samplers, and sequencers), and because they are influenced to varying degrees by hip-hop (rhythms, loops, and rapping). Some major sub-styles within urban contemporary are R&B ballad, dance/pop, and neo-soul.

R&B Ballad (1980s)

The R&B and soul ballads of the 1980s used high-gloss production to achieve a smooth and romantic sound. The Yamaha DX-7 (a popular keyboard of the time) was noted for its very bright, "digital" electric piano simulation, and this sound made its way onto many classic ballad recordings of the period. Noted R&B ballad keyboardists and artists include Robbie Buchanan and Randy Kerber (Whitney Houston), Greg Phillinganes (Mariah Carey, Anita Baker), and George Duke (Jeffrey Osbourne, Natalie Cole).

Dance/Pop (1980s/90s)

This dance style saw a return to tougher, more funk-influenced grooves, often laced with layers of electric guitars and synthesizers. Strong backbeats (often using big, sampled drum sounds) and rock riffs were also featured. Although the funk influence is predominant, not all dance/pop is considered "soulful" (particularly the more rock-influenced examples). Important dance/pop artists from this period include Prince, Michael Jackson, Janet Jackson, Bobby Brown, Madonna, and Keith Sweat.

Neo-Soul (1990s/2000s)

The term neo-soul is used to describe a fusion of 60s/70s classic soul, and 90s/00s urban and hip-hop. The classic soul influence is felt in the vocal stylings and harmonies used. The hip-hop influence derives from the rhythmic sounds (i.e. loops, samples) and overall production. Vintage electric piano sounds (as played by Alicia Keys and others) enjoy a big resurgence in this style. The vocals may include spoken-word (i.e. as in rap music) as well as more conventionally "sung" vocals, sometimes all combined in the same song (as in songs by Mariah Carey, Usher and others). Some additional important neo-soul artists include Babyface, Mary J. Blige, and Brian McKnight.

Now, we'll review the chords and scales needed to play R&B music (in Chapter 2), before focusing on keyboard voicings and comping techniques (starting in Chapter 3). On with the show!

SCALES and CHORDS

Major scales and modes

First, we'll look at the **major scale**, which is the fundamental basis of harmony in most contemporary music styles. I recommend that you think of this scale in terms of the intervals it contains—whole step, whole step, half step, whole step, whole step, whole step and half step—as this most closely parallels how the ear relates to the scale. Here is the C major scale, showing these intervals:

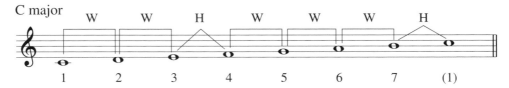

Here for your reference are all of the major scales. After C major, the next seven scales contain flats, i.e., F major has one flat, B♭ major has 2 flats, and so on. The next seven scales contain sharps, i.e., G major has one sharp, D major has 2 sharps, and so on.

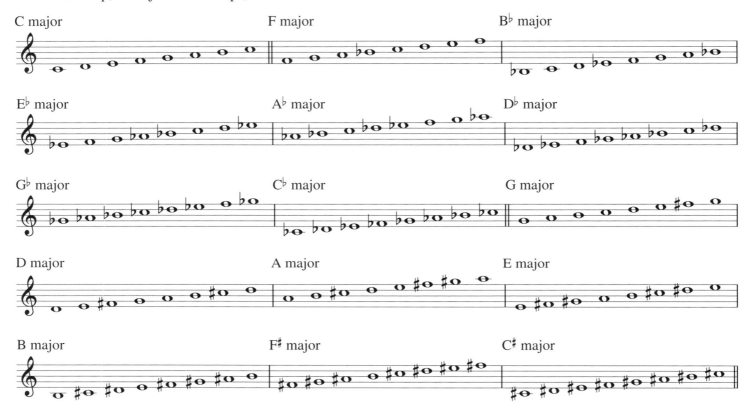

In this book, we'll work with music examples in different major and minor keys. For example, a tune will be "in the key of C major" if the note C is heard as the tonic or "home base," and if the notes used are within the C major scale (except for any sharped or flatted notes occurring in the music). Similarly, a tune will be "in the key of A minor" if the note A is heard as the tonic or "home base," and if the notes used are within an A minor scale (again, except for any sharped or flatted notes).

A **key signature** is a group of flats or sharps at the beginning of the music that lets you know which key you are in. Each key signature works for both a **major** and a **minor** key, which are considered relative to one another. For instance, the first key signature shown in the following example (no sharps and no flats) works for both the keys of C major and A minor. To find out which minor key shares the same key signature as a major key, we count up to the 6th degree of the corresponding major scale. For example, the 6th degree of a C major scale is the note A, so the keys of C major and A minor are relative to one another and share the same key signature.

Here, for your reference, are all of the major and minor key signatures:

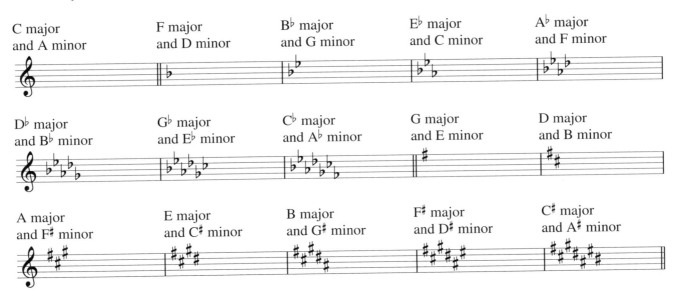

C major and A minor   F major and D minor   B♭ major and G minor   E♭ major and C minor   A♭ major and F minor

D♭ major and B♭ minor   G♭ major and E♭ minor   C♭ major and A♭ minor   G major and E minor   D major and B minor

A major and F♯ minor   E major and C♯ minor   B major and G♯ minor   F♯ major and D♯ minor   C♯ major and A♯ minor

A **mode** or modal scale is created when we take a major scale and displace it to start on another scale degree. An example of this is the **Mixolydian** mode, created when the major scale is displaced to start on the 5th degree, as in the following example of a C major scale displaced to create a G Mixolydian mode:

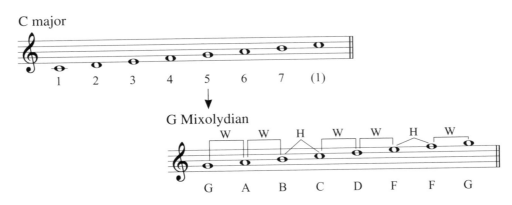

If you compare the two scales above, you'll see that the notes are the same; they just begin (and end) differently. Each has a different tonic or root, and a different pattern of whole and half steps. You can also think of the Mixolydian mode as a major scale with a flatted 7th (1–2–3–4–5–6–♭7). This mode is the basic scale source for a **dominant 7th chord** (more about these shortly), and is therefore very useful when creating parts over dominant harmonies. Another important mode in R&B styles is the **Aeolian** mode, created when the major scale is displaced to start on the 6th degree:

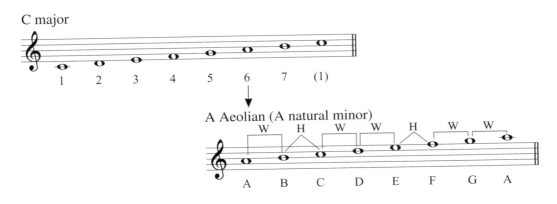

The Aeolian mode is also equivalent to the natural minor scale, which in R&B (as well as pop and rock) styles is the minor scale most commonly used in minor keys. You can also think of the Aeolian mode as a major scale with a flatted 3rd, 6th and 7th (1–2–♭3–4–5–♭6–♭7).

Pentatonic and blues scales

The **major pentatonic** scale (also known as the pentatonic scale) is a five-note scale widely used in R&B, as well as in mainstream pop and rock styles. It can be derived from the major scale by removing the 4th and 7th degrees:

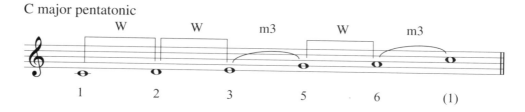

Note that from bottom to top, this scale contains the following intervals: whole step, whole step, minor 3rd, whole step, and minor 3rd. You should make it a goal to learn this very important scale in all keys.

The **minor pentatonic scale** (also known as blues pentatonic) can be derived from the major pentatonic scale. For example, if we take the C pentatonic scale and displace it to start on the note A (which is the relative minor of C), we create an A minor pentatonic scale, as follows:

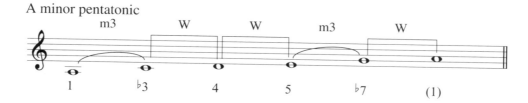

Note that from bottom to top, this scale now contains the following intervals: minor 3rd, whole step, whole step, minor 3rd, and whole step.

Finally, the **blues scale** can be derived by adding one note, the #4/♭5, to the minor pentatonic scale. For example, if we take the A minor pentatonic scale and add the connecting tone D# between the notes D and E, we create an A blues scale, as follows:

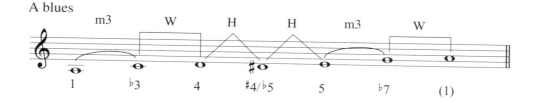

Again, you should make it a goal to learn the minor pentatonic and blues scales in all keys.

Triads and suspensions

There are four main types of triad (three-part chord) in common usage: **major**, **minor**, **augmented**, and **diminished**. The following example shows all of these triads built from the root of C:

Note that these triads are formed by building the following intervals above the root note:

Major triad:	Major 3rd and perfect 5th (1–3–5)
Minor triad:	Minor 3rd and perfect 5th (1–♭3–5)
Augmented triad:	Major 3rd and augmented 5th (1–3–♯5)
Diminished triad:	Minor 3rd and diminished 5th (1–♭3–♭5)

A **suspension** of a major or minor triad occurs when the **3rd** of the chord is replaced with another chord tone, most commonly the **4th** (also referred to as the 11th). The **9th** (also referred to as the 2nd) can also be added to a major or minor triad, either instead of or in addition to the 3rd, as follows:

Note the alternate chord symbols above the staff, which you may encounter for these chords:

*   In measure 1, we have replaced the 3rd of a major or minor triad with the 4th/11th. If "sus" is used without a number following it in the chord symbol, the 4th/11th is assumed.
*   In measure 2, we have replaced the 3rd of a major or minor triad with the 9th/2nd. Although the (add9, no3) suffix best reflects the quality of this chord, many people find the shorter "sus2" suffix more convenient.
*   In measure 3, we have added the 9th/2nd to a major triad.
*   In measure 4, we have added the 9th/2nd to a minor triad.

These are all very common sounds in more modern R&B styles.

If we construct triads from each degree of the major scale, and only use notes belonging to the scale, we create **diatonic** triads. The following example shows the diatonic triads found within the C Major scale:

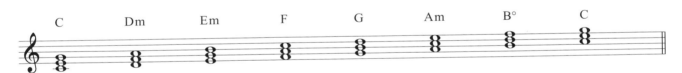

Relating the above triads to the four main triad types, note that **major** triads are built from the 1st, 4th, and 5th major scale degrees, **minor** triads are built from the 2nd, 3rd, and 6th scale degrees, and a **diminished** triad is built from the 7th scale degree. (The augmented triad does not occur anywhere in the diatonic series).

R&B songs from many different eras use diatonic triad chord progressions, so you should strive to learn these in as many keys as possible.

Seventh (four-part) chords and alterations

The term "seventh chord" is sometimes used to describe four-part chords in which the highest note or extension is the 7th. The four-part chords most commonly used in R&B are the **major 7th**, **minor 7th**, **minor 7th (♭5)**, **dominant 7th**, **suspended dominant 7th**, and **dominant 7th (♯5)** chords. The following example shows these four-part chords, built from the root of C:

Note that these chords are formed by building the following intervals above the root note:

Major 7th chord: Major 3rd, perfect 5th, and major 7th (1–3–5–7)

Minor 7th chord: Minor 3rd, perfect 5th, and minor 7th (1–♭3–5–♭7)

Minor 7♭5 chord: Minor 3rd, diminished 5th, and minor 7th (1–♭3–♭5–♭7)

Dominant 7th chord: Major 3rd, perfect 5th, and minor 7th (1–3–5–♭7)

Suspended Dominant 7th chord: Perfect 4th, perfect 5th and minor 7th (1–4–5–♭7)

Dominant 7th (♯5) chord: Major 3rd, augmented 5th and minor 7th (1–3–♯5–♭7)

If we construct four-part chords from each degree of the major scale, and stay within the restrictions of the scale, we create **diatonic** four-part chords. The following example shows the diatonic four-part chords found within the C Major scale:

Relating the above four-part chords to those previously shown, note that major 7th chords are built from the 1st and 4th major scale degrees, minor 7th chords are built from the 2nd, 3rd and 6th scale degrees, a dominant 7th chord is built from the 5th scale degree, and a minor 7th (♭5) chord is built from the 7th scale degree. (The dominant 7(♯5) chord does not occur anywhere in the diatonic series).

Many R&B tunes and progressions use these diatonic four-part chords, so you should strive to learn these in as many keys as possible.

Ninth (five-part) chords and alterations

The term "ninth chord" is sometimes used to describe five-part chords in which the highest note or extension is the 9th. The five-part chords most commonly used in R&B styles are the **major 9th**, **major 6/9**, **minor 9th**, **dominant 9th**, **suspended dominant 9th**, **dominant 7th (♯9)**, and **dominant 7th (♯5, ♯9)** chords. The following example shows these five-part chords, built from the root of C:

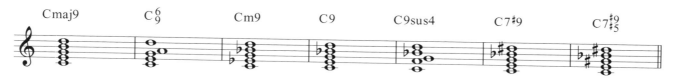

We can analyze the intervals in each of these five-part chords as follows:

Major 9th chord: Major 3rd, perfect 5th, major 7th and major 9th (1–3–5–7–9)

Major 6/9 chord: Minor 3rd, perfect 5th, major 6th and major 9th (1–3–5–6–9)

Minor 9th chord: Minor 3rd, perfect 5th, minor 7th and major 9th (1–♭3–5–♭7–9)

Dominant 9th chord: Major 3rd, perfect 5th, minor 7th and major 9th (1–3–5–♭7–9)

Suspended Dominant 9th chord: Perfect 4th, perfect 5th, minor 7th and major 9th (1–4–5–♭7–9)

Dominant 7th (♯9) chord: Major 3rd, perfect 5th, minor 7th and augmented 9th (1–3–5–♭7–♯9)

Dominant 7th (♯5,♯9) chord: Major 3rd, augmented 5th, minor 7th and augmented 9th (1–3–♯5–♭7–♯9)

In this chapter, I've tried to summarize the essential music theory and harmony that will help you play R&B styles on the keyboard. If you would like further information on these topics, please check out my other music instruction books, *Contemporary Music Theory (Levels 1-3)* and *The Pop Piano Book*. (All of these books are published by Hal Leonard Corporation.)

Chapter 3

R&B KEYBOARD HARMONY and VOICINGS

Voicing concepts

Although it is important that you know how to spell the chords described in Chapter 2, be aware that the larger the chords get (especially "ninth" chords and above), the less likely you are to "voice" them on the keyboard in simple ascending note stacks. A keyboard **voicing** is a specific allocation of notes between the hands, chosen to interpret the chord symbol in question. In other words, knowing how to spell the chords is one thing, but knowing how to voice them on the keyboard is quite another.

In R&B styles, we will often make use of **upper structure** voicings. These are three- or four-part interior chords which are in turn "built from" a chord tone (for example, 3rd, 5th, 7th etc.) of the overall chord needed. Many of the triads and four-part chords we reviewed in the last chapter, will also function as upper structures on larger chords. This is a very efficient voicing method, not least because the same upper structures can be used within various different overall chords.

Many of the voicings shown in this chapter use the upper structures in the right hand, played over the root of the overall chord in the left hand. This voicing concept is also used in Chapter 4, as we create rhythmic comping grooves for the different keyboard instruments. These upper structures can also be used in the left hand (around the middle C area) below a melody or solo in the right hand, particularly in the jazzier R&B styles.

Major and minor triad inversions

As we will shortly see, the major triad is a very commonly used upper structure on various different overall chords. Here are the inversions of a C major triad:

TRACK 1

Note that in the above example, the first triad shown is in **root position** (with the root on the bottom), the second triad is in **first inversion** (with the 3rd on the bottom), and the third triad is in **second inversion** (with the 5th on the bottom). The last triad is in root position, an octave higher than the first. To connect smoothly between successive voicings, it is important to have these inversions under your fingers in all keys. You should make it a goal to learn all the major triad inversions, as follows on the next page:

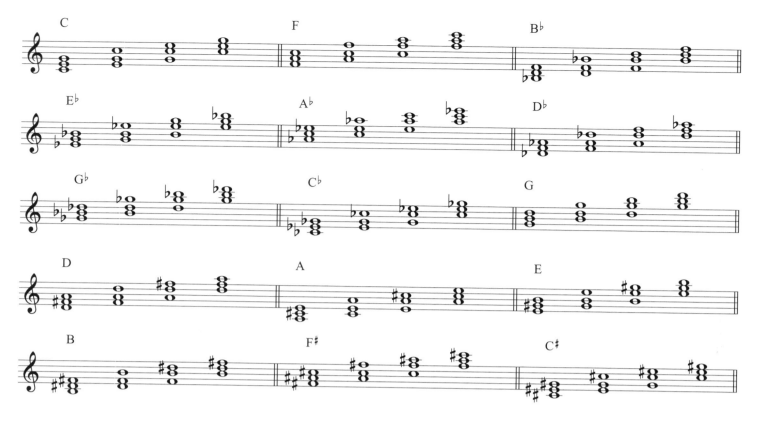

The minor triad is also very useful as an upper structure voicing. Here are the inversions of a C minor triad:

TRACK 2

The above example contains C minor triads in root position, first inversion, second inversion, and then root position again (similar to the previous major triad examples).

Again, you should learn these inversions in all keys, as shown in the following example:

Resolutions within triads

Embellishing triads with "interior resolutions" is a very effective technique across the range of pop, rock and R&B styles. The three most common resolutions used within major and minor triads are:

- The 2nd (or 9th) moving to the root

- The 2nd (or 9th) moving to the 3rd

- The 4th (or 11th) moving to the 3rd

Normally, the remaining triad tones are held down while the resolution is being played. It is very useful to get these under your fingers within all triad inversions, as follows:

TRACK 3

- In measures 1–2, the 2nd/9th (D) is resolving to the root (C), within inversions of C and Cm triads.

- In measures 3–4, the 2nd/9th (D) is resolving to the 3rd (E or E♭), within inversions of C and Cm triads.

- In measures 5–6, the 4th/11th (F) is resolving to the 3rd (E or E♭), within inversions of C and Cm triads.

This technique is especially useful when incorporated into triad-over-root voicings (see the following section, and later comping examples).

Triad-over-root chord voicings

The first upper structure technique we will present is the "triad-over-root voicing." Different rules will apply depending upon what overall type of chord (for example, major, minor, dominant etc) we are trying to create. First we will look at the commonly used triad-over-root voicings for major chords:

TRACK 4

We can make the following observations about this example, which will apply to all the upper structure voicings shown in this chapter:

- The upper structures in the right hand (triads in this case) are each "built from" different chord tones of the overall chord (from the root, 3rd, 5th, and 9th of C major in this case). Each inversion of the upper structure is shown in the right hand. The root of the overall chord is played by the left hand each time.

13

- There are two chord symbols above each measure. The first is a **slash chord** symbol, with the upper structure on the left of the slash, and the root note on the right. The second is the equivalent **composite** symbol, showing the overall chord created by placing the upper structure over the root.

- Although both "slash" and "composite" are valid chord symbol styles, you are more likely to see composite symbols in a chart or fakebook. In order to use this upper structure voicing technique, you will need to be able to derive a slash chord from a composite chord symbol. There are normally two ways in which this is done:

- **Literal translation**: using an upper structure voicing which when placed over the root, is exactly equivalent to the composite symbol. For example, if you see the chord symbol Cmaj7 and you respond with the second voicing shown (Em/C), you have exactly created a Cmaj7 chord between the hands, with no additional notes.

- **Upgrading**: using an upper structure voicing, which when placed over the root, adds more notes/extensions to the composite symbol. For example, if you see the chord symbol Cmaj7 and you respond with the third voicing shown (G/C), you have added the 9th (and also removed the 3rd). While not appropriate in all situations, this type of upgrade can often sound very cool!

Now we will analyze these specific major-chord voicings as follows:

- In the first measure, we are building a major triad from the root of the overall major chord (C/C). This is a simple triad-over-root voicing, which creates a basic major chord.

- In the second measure, we are building a minor triad from the 3rd of the overall major chord (Em/C). This creates a major seventh chord overall.

- In the third measure, we are building a major triad from the 5th of the overall major chord (G/C). This creates a major ninth chord, with the 3rd omitted.

- In the fourth measure, we are building a major triad from the 9th of the overall major chord (D/C). This creates a major six-nine chord, with a sharped 11th (F♯ in this case).

Play each of these voicings to get the sounds in your ears, and the shapes under your fingers! Next we will look at triad-over-root voicings for minor chords:

TRACK 5

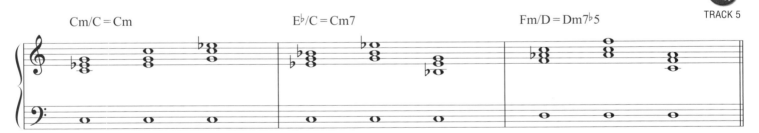

Cm/C = Cm   E♭/C = Cm7   Fm/D = Dm7♭5

We can analyze these chord voicings as follows:

- In the first measure, we are building a minor triad from the root of the overall minor chord (Cm/C). This is a simple triad-over-root voicing which creates a basic minor chord.

- In the second measure, we are building a major triad from the 3rd of the overall minor chord (E♭/C). This creates a minor seventh chord overall. (Note that E♭ is a minor third interval above the root of C).

- In the third measure, we are building a minor triad from the 3rd of the overall minor chord (Fmi/D). This creates a minor seventh with flatted 5th chord overall. (Note that F is a minor third interval above the root of D).

Again, there are voicing upgrade possibilities here. For example, it is common practice in many R&B styles to upgrade basic minor triad chord symbols by building the major triad from the 3rd, creating a minor 7th chord overall. Next, we will look at triad-over-root voicings for dominant and suspended dominant chords:

TRACK 6

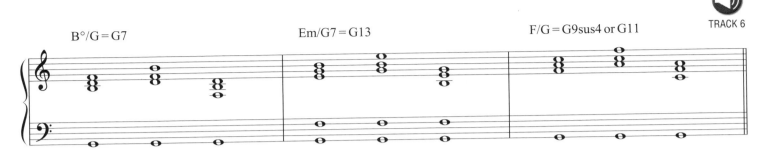

We can analyze these chord voicings as follows:

- In the first measure, we are building a diminished triad from the 3rd of the overall dominant chord (B°/G). This creates a dominant seventh chord overall.

- In the second measure, we are building a minor triad from the 13th (same as the 6th) of the overall dominant chord (Em/G7), with the left hand playing the root and 7th below. This creates a dominant 13th chord (in this case, by adding the 13th to the dominant 7th) overall.

- In the third measure, we are building a major triad from the 7th of the overall suspended dominant chord (F/G). This creates a suspended dominant ninth (also known as a dominant eleventh) chord. (Note that F is a minor seventh interval above the root of G). The term "suspended" means that the 3rd of the dominant chord (B) has been replaced by the 4th/11th (C). This voicing can also work as a less defined or "incomplete" minor 11th chord.

Now we'll see how to move between chords using these voicings and inversions. This progression has been voiced using the triad-over-root method:

TRACK 7
part 1

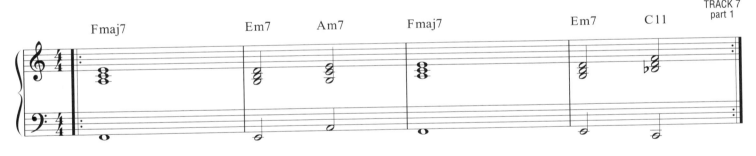

Note that we no longer have the slash chord symbols above the staff - just the composite symbols (a realistic situation when we are interpreting a chart or fake book). We need to look at each of these symbols and derive a triad-over-root voicing for each one. Then we need to **voice lead** smoothly between these upper structure triads, by using inversions to avoid unnecessary interval skips. We can summarize the voicing choices as follows:

- In measures 1 and 3, the Fmaj7 chord is voiced by building a minor triad from the 3rd (Am/F).

- In measures 2 and 4, the Em7 chord is voiced by building a major triad from the 3rd (G/E).

- In measure 2, the Am7 chord is voiced by building a major triad from the 3rd (C/A).

- In measure 4, the C11 chord is voiced by building a major triad from the flatted 7th (B♭/C).

Now we will apply a sixteenth-note rhythm pattern to these voicings:

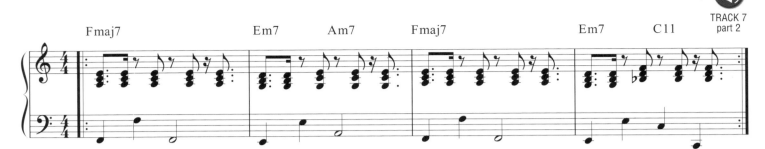

This creates a typical R&B comping pattern. Note the "funky" right-hand syncopations on the last 16th note of beat 1, and the second 16th note of beat 4, in each measure.

Alternating triad chord voicings

"Alternating triads" involves the use of two different upper structure triads over the same bass note, for the duration of a particular chord. This is a common pop-rock keyboard technique which is also applicable in various R&B situations. You'll recognize many of these upper structures from the preceding triad-over-root text. The following example contains the commonly-used alternating triad voicings for major, minor and dominant chords:

We can analyze the above table of alternating triad options as follows:

- Measures 1–5 contain the alternating triad pairs for major chords: IV–I, V–I, II–I, ii–I, and iii–vi.

- Measures 6–8 contain the alternating triad pairs for minor chords: ♭VII–♭III, ♭III–IV, and ♭III–♭VI.

- Measure 9 contains the alternating triad pair for dominant/suspended chords: ♭VII–I.

It should be noted that Roman numerals will be used throughout this book in two basic ways:

1) At the bottom of the previous page, the numerals are used to show the position or interval of a chord above a particular bass note. In describing measure 1 of Track 8, note that an F major triad lies a fourth above the C bass note. Since the triad is major, an upper-case Roman numeral is used (lower-case for minor). Also, the note F is a perfect fourth above C, equivalent to being the fourth pitch in the C major scale, thus we use the plain numeral without an accidental in front of it. In describing measure 6 of Track 8, a flat symbol is placed in front of the numerals VII and III to label the triads above the bass-note D. Since C♯ would be the seventh note in the D major scale, and we have a *C natural* triad, the ♭VII shows that we are forming a triad from a note a half-step lower than what would be the seventh pitch in the major scale, above the bass note. In other words, the note C is a minor 7th interval above the bass note D.

2) In traditional harmonic analysis, Roman numerals are use to label the position or function of chords within a specific key. These positions are based on scale degrees. For example, in the key of C major, a G chord would be labeled V since its root is the fifth scale degree in the key. The common chord progression I–IV–V would involve the C, F, and G chords.

* Be aware that when discussing alternating triad voicings, Roman numeral method 1) will be used. In discussions of chord progressions within specific keys, 2) will be used.

Next we will look at a chord progression example, voiced using alternating triads:

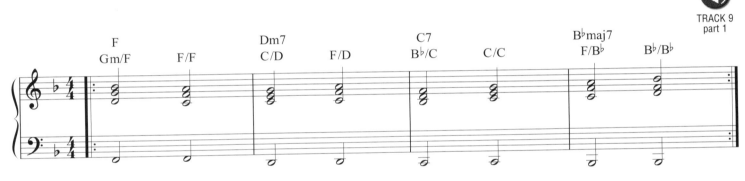

Note that two lines of chord symbols are shown above this example. The top line (F, Dm7 etc.) contains the main chord symbols as you might see on a chart in a fake book. The second line (Gm/F, F/F etc.) shows the result of interpreting the first line with some of the alternating triad voicings in the preceding example. Various choices are available, and of course, you are encouraged to experiment. In commercial R&B styles, we would normally choose upper triads which stay within the key of the song, and support the melody if present. The above alternating triad choices are further explained as follows:

• In measure 1, the F chord is interpreted with ii–I alternating triads (Gm to F) over the bass note of F.

• In measure 2, the Dm7 chord is interpreted with ♭VII–♭III alternating triads (C to F) over the bass note of D.

• In measure 3, the C7 chord is interpreted with ♭VII–I alternating triads (B♭ to C) over the bass note of C.

• In measure 4, the B♭maj7 chord is interpreted with V–I alternating triads (F to B♭) over the bass note of B♭.

Now we will apply a swing-sixteenth rhythm pattern to these voicings:

This pattern would work for the more modern swing-sixteenth funk or hip-hop styles. Note the right hand anticipations of beat 3, and the rhythmic "conversation" between the hands (around beat 2)—all commonly used funk keyboard devices. Have fun coming up with your own patterns using alternating triads!

Mixolydian third intervals and triads

Next, we will explore using intervals and triads from Mixolydian modes to create comping patterns and fills. This is primarily a blues piano technique, one which has been incorporated into various R&B styles. As the Mixolydian mode is a basic scale source for a dominant 7th chord, these patterns are well suited to the dominant chord progressions often found in blues and R&B. Grace notes which are a half-step below the the 3rd and/or 5th of the dominant chord can then be added for a "bluesy" effect. All of the following patterns create or imply a G7 chord:

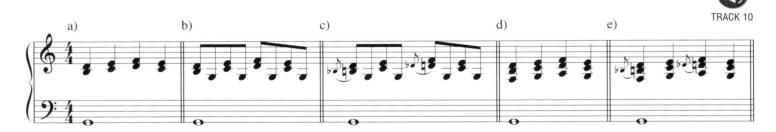

- Pattern a) uses the third intervals with the top notes of the 5th, 6th, and 7th of the implied G7 chord—these are the most commonly used "Mixolydian 3rd" intervals used in blues and R&B.

- Pattern b) is a variation which adds the root of the G7 on all the upbeats.

- Pattern c) adds the grace notes B♭ before the B (♭3–3) and D♭ before the D (♭5–5).

- Pattern d) expands these intervals to second-inversion "Mixolydian triads," again with the same top notes, resulting in B°, C, and Dm triads, all over the implied G7 chord.

- Pattern e) adds the half-step grace notes to these Mixolydian triads. All of these are signature sounds in blues, blues-rock, and R&B.

Left hand open triad arpeggios

Building "open triad" arpeggio patterns in the left hand is a staple R&B ballad technique, one that is also used in pop, rock, and country ballads. An open triad is a three-note chord in which the middle note has been raised by an octave. For example, an F major triad would be spelled F–A–C from bottom to top. If we then take the note A and transpose it up an octave, we get the F–C–A sequence shown at the start of patterns a) and c) below. Had the triad not been "opened" in this way, the arpeggio (with the sustain pedal used) would sound muddy and indistinct in the lower register. The open triad however, sounds broad and clear and gives good support below right-hand melody or comping. Open triad patterns can be used within 8th- and 16th-note rhythmic styles, and can add more extensions to the chord (in addition to the root, 3rd, and 5th) once the left hand has moved up to the middle C area, as in the following examples:

TRACK 11

- Pattern a) uses an eighth-note open triad pattern (root-5th-3rd) on the F major chord, with the 5th repeated on the "and" of 2.

- Pattern b) is a variation which adds the 9th of the chord (G) before the 3rd.

- Pattern c) uses a sixteenth-note open triad pattern (root-5th-3rd) on both the F major and D minor chords, with the 5th played on the last 16th of beats 1 and 3 respectively.

- Pattern d) is a busier variation which adds the 9th (G) and 6th (D) of the F major chord. We will see various uses of this left-hand open triad technique, in the later comping examples.

Pentatonic scale fills, and use over chords

Pentatonic scales are a very useful source of fills and patterns across a wide range of R&B, rock, and country styles. These fills often use sustained or repeated top notes (sometimes called "drones") which are normally the tonic or 5th of the scale, above interval movements from the same scale, as follows:

TRACK 12

In the first measure above, we have a reminder of the C pentatonic scale. In the second measure, we have two phrases using the 5th (G) as a drone, or top note, above the whole-step movement of D–E or E–D, and then ending on C. In the third measure, we have two phrases using the tonic (C) as a "drone," or top note, above the whole-step movement of G–A or A–G, and then ending on E. In the more modern R&B styles, these phrasings are especially useful when the pentatonic scale is in turn built from a chord tone such as the 3rd, 5th, or 7th, as in the following example:

TRACK 13

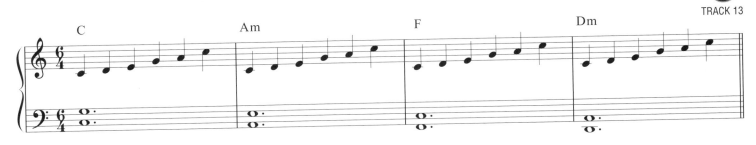

In the preceding example, the C pentatonic scale has been "built from" the root of a C major chord, the 3rd of an A minor chord, the 5th of an F major chord, and the 7th of a D minor chord. Note that more chord extensions are added as we go from left-to-right in this example. In summary we can "build" pentatonic scales from the root and 5th of major chords, and from the 3rd and 7th of minor chords. Building the pentatonic from the 7th will also work on suspended dominant chords. Patterns such as those in Track 12 will also work over the above chords, and you are of course encouraged to experiment! We will see several instances of this pentatonic scale "building" in later examples.

Major and minor seventh chord inversions

The major 7th four-part chord is another useful upper structure on some larger chords. Here are the inversions of a C major seventh chord:

TRACK 14

Note that in the above example, the first chord shown is in **root position** (with the root on the bottom), the second chord is in **first inversion** (with the 3rd on the bottom), the third chord is in **second inversion** (with the 5th on the bottom), and the fourth chord is in third inversion (with the 7th on the bottom). The first inversion major seventh chord sounds more dissonant due to the "exposed" half-step interval on top, and this inversion therefore needs to be used with some care. You should make it a goal to learn all the major seventh chord inversions, as follows:

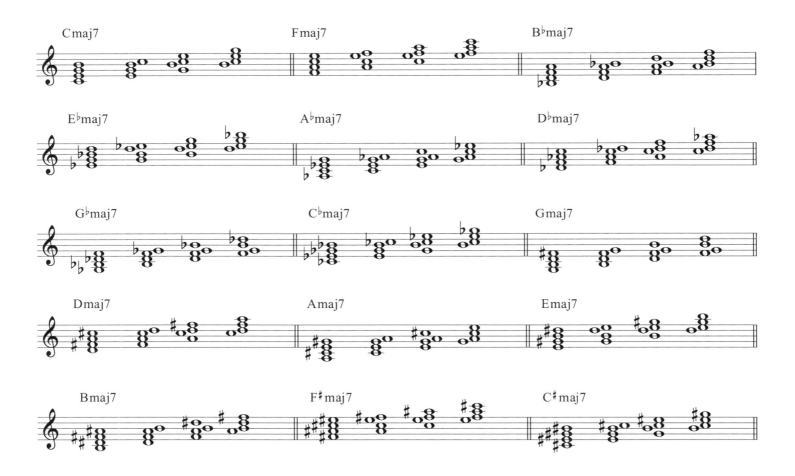

The minor 7th four-part chord, like the major 7th, is also a useful upper structure on larger chords. Here are the inversions of a C minor seventh chord:

TRACK 15

The above example contains C minor 7th chords in root position, first inversion, second inversion, and third inversion (similar to the previous major 7th chord examples).

Again, you should learn these inversions in all keys, as shown in the following example:

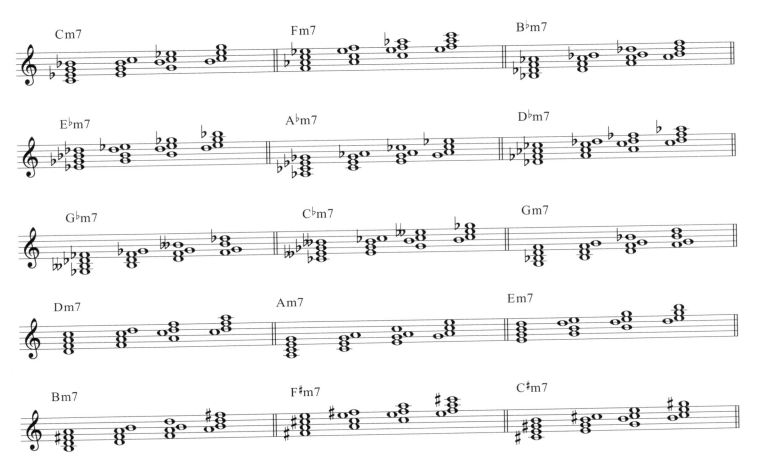

We saw in Chapter 2 that a minor 7th chord can be altered to a minor 7th ($\flat$5) chord, by lowering the 5th. The minor 7th ($\flat$5) chord is a useful upper structure when voicing dominant harmonies. Here are the first three m7($\flat$5) chords and inversions around the circle-of-5ths, and it is again recommended that you become familiar with these in all keys:

TRACK 16

Four-part-over-root chord voicings

The next upper structure technique we will look at is the "four-part-over-root" voicing. This involves building a four-part interior chord from a chord tone (3rd, 5th, 7th, etc.) of the overall chord. Again, different rules will apply depending upon what type of chord (major, minor, dominant, etc.) we are trying to create. First, we will look at the commonly used four-part-over-root voicings for major and minor chords:

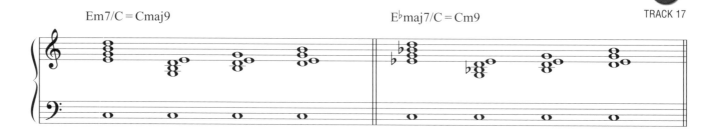

TRACK 17

Note that (as for the triad-over-root voicings), both slash chord and composite chord symbols are shown, and all inversions of the upper structures are shown. Again, the goal is to be able to interpret the composite symbol with a suitable upper structure voicing. We can analyze the above voicings as follows:

- In the first measure, we are building a minor 7th four-part chord from the 3rd of the overall major chord (Em7/C). This creates a major ninth chord overall.

- In the second measure, we are building a major 7th four-part chord from the 3rd of the overall minor chord ($E\flat$maj7/C). This creates a minor ninth chord overall. (Note that $E\flat$ is a minor third interval above the root of C).

Again, it is fairly common practice in R&B styles to upgrade major 7th chord symbols by using the first voicing above, and to upgrade minor 7th chord symbols by using the second voicing above. In both cases, the net result is to add the 9th of the chord. In some cases, we might even upgrade basic major and minor triad symbols this way (which would then add the 7th and 9th) to provide more density and sophistication, if needed.

Next, we have some four-part-over-root voicings for dominant and suspended dominant chords:

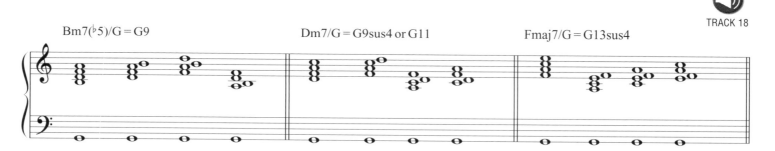

TRACK 18

We can analyze these voicings as follows:

- In the first measure, we are building a minor 7th ($\flat$5) four-part chord from the 3rd of the overall dominant chord (Bm7($\flat$5)/G). This creates a dominant ninth chord overall.

- In the second measure, we are building a minor 7th four-part chord from the 5th of the overall suspended dominant chord (Dm7/G). This creates a suspended dominant ninth (or dominant eleventh) chord overall.

- In the third measure, we are building a major 7th four-part chord from the 7th of the overall suspended dominant chord (Fmaj7/G). This creates a suspended dominant thirteenth chord overall.

Now we'll see how to move between chords using these voicings and inversions. This progression has been voiced using the four-part-over-root method:

TRACK 19
part 1

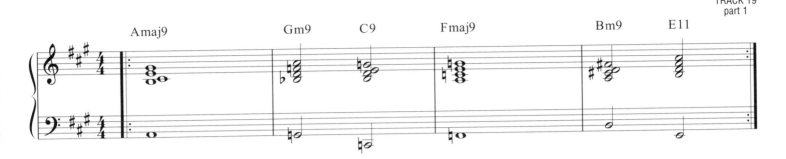

Again, we are showing the composite chord symbols, and our job is to interpret these with suitable upper-structure voicings and inversions, which are analyzed as follows:

- In the first measure, the Amaj9 chord is voiced by building a minor 7th four-part chord from the 3rd (C#mi7/A).

- In the second measure (beat 1), the Gm9 chord is voiced by building a major 7th four-part chord from the 3rd (B♭maj7/G).

- In the second measure (beat 3), the C9 chord is voiced by building a minor 7th (♭5) four-part chord from the 3rd (Em7♭5/C).

- In the third measure, the Fmaj9 chord is voiced by building a minor 7th four-part chord from the 3rd (Ami7/F).

- In the fourth measure (beat 1), the Bm9 chord is voiced by building a major 7th four-part chord from the 3rd (Dmaj7/B).

- In the fourth measure (beat 3), the E11 chord is voiced by building a minor 7th four-part chord from the 5th (Bm7/E).

Now we can apply an R&B rhythmic "comping" pattern to these voicings:

TRACK 19
part 2

Note the 16th-note anticipation of beat 3 in all the left-hand measures and in the 2nd and 4th right-hand measures. The right hand voicings also create a syncopated pattern by landing on the "and" of 3 and on the 2nd 16th-note of beat 4, in the first and third measures. These are all signature rhythmic patterns across a range of R&B styles.

Seven-three chord voicings

The seven-three voicing is a staple jazz piano technique which is also useful in some R&B and blues styles. It involves playing only the seventh and third of the chord, which are the definitive "color" tones of any four-part chord, as in the following example:

TRACK 20
part 1

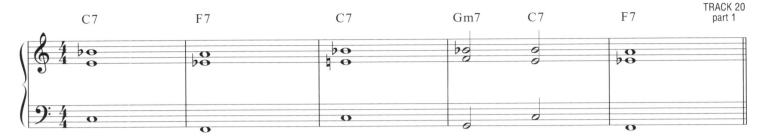

Again we can apply a rhythmic comping pattern to these seven-three voicings. This example uses eighth-note anticipations, suitable for a 50s/60s blues-influenced R&B groove:

TRACK 20
part 2

Pentatonic patterns using fourth intervals

The next technique uses perfect fourth intervals from the minor pentatonic scale, and is often used in minor keys across a range of rock, R&B, and funk styles. The example below uses 4th intervals from an E minor pentatonic scale, and places them over the bass notes of E, G, A, B, C, and D. In the implied key of E minor, the chord qualities created are i, III, iv, v, VI and VII respectively. These are commonly used bass notes and chord qualities in minor keys, in the more commercial rock and R&B styles:

TRACK 21
part 1

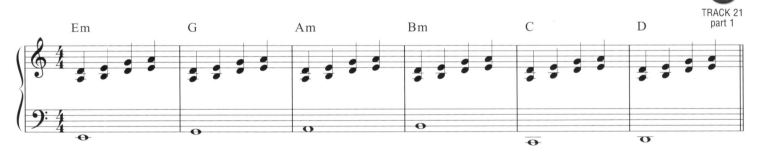

Well-known examples of this voicing technique include the R&B/funk tune "Superstition" by Stevie Wonder, and the pop-rock tune "That's All" by Genesis. Here's a sixteenth-note funk comping pattern using these fourth intervals, reminiscent of the tune "Superstition":

TRACK 21
part 2

Double 4th/Cluster shapes and chord voicings

The next voicing technique in this chapter uses what I call "double 4th" and cluster shapes. I use the term "shape" when referring to these, as (unlike the triad and four-part voicings earlier in this chapter) they are not easily or helpfully described with individual chord symbols. Double 4ths are three-note voicings created by stacking two perfect 4th intervals on top of one another, and can be varied with inversions and octave doubling. Clusters are three-note voicings containing a whole-step or half-step at the bottom. Here are the commonly-used double 4ths and clusters in the more modern R&B styles:

TRACK 22

In the first measure, we begin with a root-position double 4th (D–G–C). After this, the shape is then shown in first and second inversions. In the second measure, we start by combining the first and second inversions together ("doubling" the G an octave below), and then we combine the second inversion and root position (doubling the C an octave below). In the third measure we have cluster shapes with a half-step and then a whole-step at the bottom, within a fourth interval in total. In the last measure we have a variation with a half-step at the bottom, below a fifth interval. These are all useful sounds in modern R&B, as well as contemporary jazz and new age styles. Now we'll create "double-4th-over-root" voicings for major, minor and suspended dominant chords:

TRACK 23

C		C/E	Dm7	G7sus4

We can analyze the above voicings as follows:

- In the first measure, we are building double 4ths from the 9th, 3rd, and 6th of the overall major chord. These voicings upgrade the basic C major chord symbol by adding the 9th and 6th.

- In the second measure, we are building a double 4th from the 9th of the major chord, and inverting this over the 3rd in the left hand. (This is also equivalent to an Em7♯5 chord).

- In the third measure, we are building a double 4ths from the 4th/11th and root of the overall minor chord. These voicings upgrade the Dm7 chord symbol by adding the 4th/11th.

- In the fourth measure, we are building double 4ths from the root and 5th of the overall suspende dominant chord.

Next, we'll create cluster-over-root voicings for major, minor, and suspended dominant chords:

TRACK 24

C		C/E	Dm7	G7sus4

We can analyze the preceding voicings as follows:

- In the first measure, we are building clusters with an overall span of a fourth interval (see Track 22, measure 3) from the 9th, 5th, 6th, and 7th of the overall major chord. These voicings upgrade the basic C major chord symbol by adding the 9th, 6th, and 7th.

- In the second measure, we are building the cluster variation with a half-step below a fifth interval (see Track 22 measure 4) from the 7th of the major chord, and inverting this over the 3rd in the left hand.

- In the third measure, we are building clusters with an overall span of a fourth interval from the 9th, 4th/11th, and 7th, and the cluster with a half-step below a fifth interval from the 9th, of the overall minor chord. These voicings upgrade the Dm7 chord symbol by adding the 9th and 4th/11th.

- In the fourth measure, we are building a cluster with a whole-step at the bottom and an overall span of a fourth interval, from the 4th/11th of the overall suspended dominant chord.

Next, we will use double-4th-over-root and cluster-over-root voicings over the following progression:

TRACK 25
part 1

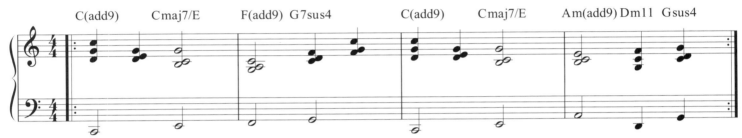

Note that although more detailed chord symbols have been used to reflect the extensions added, these upper structures are often used to upgrade more basic symbols. We can analyze the above voicings as follows:

- In the first and third measures, we are building double 4ths and clusters from the 9th of the C(add9) chord, and a cluster (half-step below a 5th) from the 7th of the Cmaj7/E chord.

- In the second measure, we are building a cluster from the 9th of the F(add9) chord, and a cluster and inverted double 4th from the 4th/11th and root of the G7sus chord, respectively.

- In the fourth measure, we are building a cluster from the 9th of the Am(add9) chord, a double 4th from the 4th/11th of the Dm7 chord, and an inverted double 4th from the 5th of the G7sus chord.

These voicings might then be used in a swing-eighths R&B/shuffle groove as follows:

TRACK 25
part 2

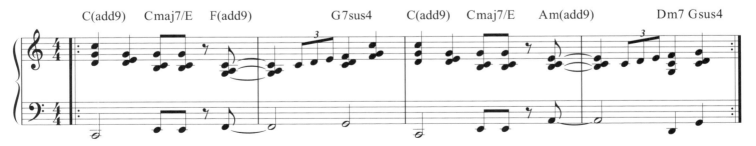

Descending fills with triads and sixth intervals

The last device we will look at is the use of diminished triads and sixth intervals, moving in a chromatically descending manner (down by successive half-steps). This can be an effective device in "turnaround" sections and in linking between chord changes, as follows:

TRACK 26

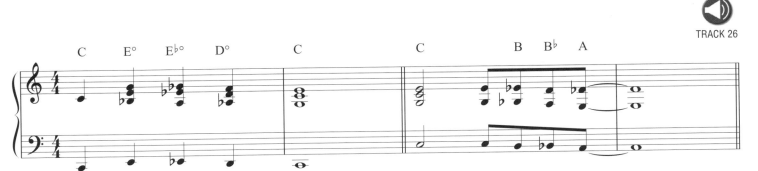

In the first two measures, the diminished triads E°, E♭°, and D° are connecting between the C chords. In the last two measures, the sixth intervals and root notes create a descending run between the C and A chords.

Chapter 4

R&B KEYBOARD COMPING STYLES

Now we get to apply the keyboard harmony covered in Chapter 3, to create authentic comping patterns in a wide variety of R&B styles. We begin by reviewing the rhythmic subdivisions used in R&B.

Rhythmic concepts

Most R&B styles are written in 4/4 time and use patterns based around eighth or sixteenth notes. Each of these subdivisions can be played **straight** or **swing**, essentially resulting in four main rhythmic styles or groups:

- Straight eighths
- Swing eighths
- Straight sixteenths
- Swing sixteenths

In a straight eighths feel, each eighth note is of equal length and divides the beat exactly in half, as follows:

Straight eighth notes

TRACK 27
part 1

Note the rhythmic counting above the staff—this is how eighth note rhythms are normally counted, with the 1, 2, 3 and 4 falling on the **downbeats**, and the "ands" falling halfway in between, on the **upbeats**.

In a swing eighths feel, the second eighth note in each beat (the "and" in the rhythmic counting) lands two-thirds of the way through the beat. This is equivalent to playing on the first and third parts of an eighth-note triplet. We still count using "1 and 2 and" etc., but now each "and" is played a little later:

Swing eighth notes

TRACK 27
part 2

Note that the first measure above looks the same as the previous straight eighths example, but when a swing eighths interpretation is applied, it sounds equivalent to the second measure above (the quarter-eighth triplets). However, as the second measure above is more cumbersome to write and to read, it is common practice to notate as in the first measure above, but to rhythmically interpret in a swing eighths style as needed.

There will also be times when we need to land on all three parts of an eighth-note triplet. In this case, the swing eighths rhythmic interpretation will not work, as this only allows us to access the first and third parts of the triplet. Instead, we either need to use eighth-note triplet signs in 4/4 time, or use 12/8 time which "exposes" all of the eighth notes without the need for triplet signs. The following example shows these two different notation styles:

Eighth-note triplets vs. 12/8 time

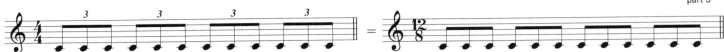

In the first measure above, each beat is divided in three equal parts. In the second measure, the time signature allows for twelve eighth notes in the measure, but we still subjectively hear four "big beats" at the start of each beamed group of eighth notes. The two measures above are therefore functionally equivalent to one another. As a general rule, I would suggest notating in 4/4 time unless there are a lot of eighth-note triplet signs needed (as in some doo-wop-influenced R&B styles for instance), making it less cumbersome to notate in 12/8 time.

As mentioned earlier, gospel music has been a major influence on R&B. Many R&B/gospel and pop/gospel songs use a 6/4 time signature, with eighth-note triplets, as follows:

6/4 time with eighth-note triplets

In this time signature, we subjectively hear two "big beats" at a slow tempo, at the start of the first and fourth beamed groups of eighth notes (often with a backbeat on the start of the fourth group). If we apply a "swing eighths" feel within this 6/4 time, any pairs of eighth notes (not written with triplet signs) would then sound like quarter-eighth triplets. This is a common notation mix in this style (see Tracks 48 and 49 later in this chapter). You may sometimes see this style written in 3/4 time instead of 6/4, in which case the number of measures would be doubled.

Returning to 4/4 time, we will now look at rhythms using sixteenth notes. In a sixteenth-note feel, all the "ands" or eighth-note upbeats will fall exactly half-way between the downbeats. However, each eighth-note will now be subdivided differently, when comparing straight sixteenth and swing sixteenth rhythmic feels. In a straight sixteenth feel, each sixteenth note is of equal length and divides the eighth-note exactly in half (and the beat exactly into quarters) as follows:

Straight sixteenth notes

Note the rhythmic counting above the staff—this is how sixteenth note rhythms are normally counted. In between the beat numbers (1, 2, 3, 4) and the "ands," we have the "e" on the 2nd sixteenth note within each beat, and the "a" on the 4th sixteenth note within each beat.

In a swing sixteenths feel, the 2nd and 4th sixteenth notes in each beat (the "e" and "a" in the rhythmic counting) land two-thirds of the way through each eighth-note, rather than dividing it in half. This is equivalent to playing on the first and third parts of an sixteenth-note triplet. We still count using "1 e & a" etc., but now each "e" and "a" is played a little later:

Swing sixteenth notes

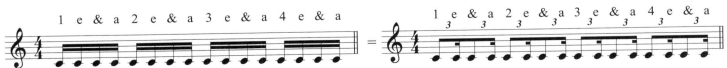

Note that the first measure in the preceding example looks the same as Track 27, part 5, but when a swing sixteenths interpretation is applied to it, it sounds equivalent to the second measure (the eighth-sixteenth triplets).

Now we will look at various comping styles and progressions for the keyboard, throughout the different eras of R&B. In each case, I have briefly summarized the rhythms and voicings used. If necessary, please refer back to Chapter 3 to review the R&B voicing techniques as you work through the comping styles.

The play-along CD contains two tracks for each of these examples. The first track is keyboard only (either acoustic piano, electric piano, organ, clavinet, or analog synth), with the left-hand part on the left channel, the right hand part on the right channel, and the hi-hat quarter-note click in the middle. This enables you to practice these examples "hands separately" by turning down one channel or the other. The second track has an R&B rhythm section on the left channel, and the keyboard part (left and right hands) on the right channel. To play along with the band on these examples, turn down the right channel.

Early R&B (50s)

We'll start with a swing eighths comping pattern in the style of "Searching" by the 50s R&B band, the Coasters. This uses an acoustic piano and rhythmically alternates between the left and right hands, using triad-over-root voicings and grace notes. The left hand pattern is based around the roots and 5ths of the chords, with some diatonic walkups (G–A–B–C):

Comping pattern #1 – Style of "Searching" by The Coasters

TRACK 28
keyboard only

TRACK 29
keyboard plus
rhythm section

Note the triad-over-root voicings in this example: the C triad built from the root of the C major chords, the F and C triads built from the 7th of the G11 and D11 chords respectively, and the B diminished triad built from the 3rd of the G7 chords. Half-step grace notes approaching the 3rds of the C and G7 chords add a "bluesy" quality.

Next, we have a straight eighths pattern in the style of "What'd I Say" by Ray Charles. This uses a Wurlitzer electric piano which was one of his signature sounds. The progression is a 12-bar blues in C, typical of early R&B styles. First, the left hand establishes the bass pattern using Mixolydian modes built from C, F and G, and then the right hand joins in using 3rd interval patterns from the same modes:

Comping pattern #2 – Style of "What'd I Say" by Ray Charles

A melodic phrase from the C blues scale has been used over the F7 chord in measure 22, and diminished triads descending by half-step have been used to lead into the C chord in measure 24. The final C7 voicing uses an E diminished triad built from the 3rd of the C7 chord.

The next example is a swing eighths pattern in the style of "Telegram" by Vernon Green and the Medallions, an important doo-wop group of the period. This uses acoustic piano and is based on triad-over-root voicings:

Comping pattern #3 – Style of "Telegram" by Vernon Green and the Medallions

TRACK 32
keyboard only

TRACK 33
keyboard plus
rhythm section

The left hand is playing the chord roots using a repeated "dotted-quarter and eighth" rhythmic pattern. The right hand upper structures are basic major or minor triads built from the root, except for the C♯ diminished triad built from the 3rd of the A7 chords. Beginning in measure 5, some upper triads are arpeggiated using eighth-note triplets, which imparts a higher energy level to the second half of this example.

Motown Soul (60s)

Our first Motown example is a straight eighths comping pattern in the style of "Heard It Through the Grapevine" by Marvin Gaye. This was recorded using a Rhodes electric piano, and uses upper triad and 4th-interval voicings:

Comping pattern #4 – Style of "Heard It Through the Grapevine" by Marvin Gaye

TRACK 34
keyboard only

TRACK 35
keyboard plus
rhythm section

The left hand quarter notes provide a steady, driving pulse to this groove. In measures 1–4 the right hand is playing upper 4th-interval voicings, mostly from the D minor pentatonic scale over the Dm7 chord. In measures 5–8 the right hand is using different inversions of ♭III–IV alternating triads (F and G major) over the Dm7 chord. In measures 9–10 we are building diminished triads from the 3rds of the dominant 7th chords (C#° on the A7, and B° on the G7), with half-step grace notes leading up to the 3rd in each case.

Next up we have a straight sixteenths pattern in the style of "I Can't Get Next To You" by the Temptations. This was recorded with acoustic piano, and again, uses a mix of upper triad and 4th-interval voicings:

Comping pattern #5 – Style of "I Can't Get Next to You" by The Temptations

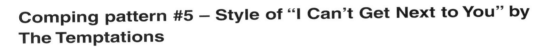

TRACK 36
keyboard only

TRACK 37
keyboard plus
rhythm section

The right-hand intro phrase in measure 1 is derived from the A blues scale. Then the main groove uses 4th intervals from the A minor pentatonic scale over the Am7 chord, underpinned with root notes in octaves in the left hand. Major triads are built from the roots of the C and D major chords, towards the end of the 2-measure phrase.

Our last Motown example is an uptempo, swing eighths pattern in the style of "My Guy" by Mary Wells. This was recorded using electric organ, and uses triad-over-root, alternating triad, and four-part-over-root voicings:

Comping pattern #6 – Style of "My Guy" by Mary Wells

TRACK 38
keyboard only

TRACK 39
keyboard plus
rhythm section

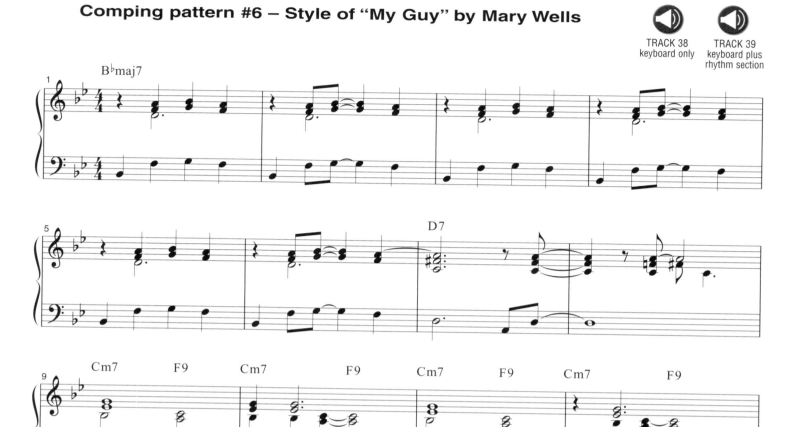

In measures 1–6 and 15, the right hand is using iii–vi alternating triads (D minor and G minor) over the B♭maj7 chord. In measures 7–8, we are building an F♯ diminished triad from the 3rd of the D7 chords, with a ♭3–3 movement in measure 8. In measures 9–16, the minor 7th chords are all voiced by building major triads from the 3rds. On the dominant 9ths (F9), we are building minor 7th(♭5) four-part shapes from the 3rd. The F7 in measure 14 is voiced simply with a dominant 7th built from the root. Note that on some right hand voicings, the upper notes are held above moving parts below, which is ideally suited for organ-based comping styles.

Memphis Soul (60s)

Next, we'll look at some soul examples from the Stax/Volt/Atlantic period – typically more raw and harder edged than the pop-oriented Motown sound. First, we have a straight eighths pattern in the style of "Sittin' on the Dock of the Bay" by Otis Redding. This uses an acoustic piano, and a mix of upper triad, interval, and pentatonic voicings:

Comping pattern #7 – Style of "Sittin' on the Dock of the Bay" by Otis Redding

TRACK 40
keyboard only

TRACK 41
keyboard plus
rhythm section

In this example, the triad-over-root voicings are either major triads built from the roots of major chords, or diminished triads built from the 3rd of dominant chords. Sixth intervals moving by successive half-steps are used to connect between the upper triads in measures 3–4, 6–7, 7–8, and 15–16, and fills using the G pentatonic scale are used to embellish the comping over the G major chords in measures 5, 9, and 13. The left hand is generally playing the chord roots on beats 1 and 3 (or the anticipation of beat 3), with some added eighth note "pickups."

Next, we have a swing eighths pattern in the style of "Green Onions" by Booker T. and the MG's. This example uses an electric organ which was a signature sound for this particular band. The chord progression is a variation on a 12-bar blues, and the voicings are a mix of 4th intervals and triads:

Comping pattern #8 – Style of "Green Onions"
by Booker T. and the MG's

TRACK 42
keyboard only

TRACK 43
keyboard plus
rhythm section

The overall form of this tune is a minor 12-bar blues; however, instead of staying on a Cm or Cm7 chord for the first four measures, we instead move from C to E♭ and F in measures 1 and 3, and from C to B♭ and back to C in measures 2 and 4. This pattern is then transposed to start on the F chord in measure 5, and so on. Although we are in the key of C minor overall, we have used major triad symbols (including C) as a "default" when the 3rd of the chord is not present. Most of the voicings use 4th intervals from the C, F and G minor pentatonic scales, with the notes arpeggiated in the first half of each measure and played together in the second half (except for the ending phrase in measure 12).

Our last Memphis soul example is a straight eighths pattern in the style of "Mustang Sally" by Wilson Pickett, a tune with a significant blues and rock 'n' roll influence. This example uses an acoustic piano and various Mixolydian devices typical of the blues, over a 12-bar blues progression in C:

Comping pattern #9 – Style of "Mustang Sally" by Wilson Pickett

TRACK 44
keyboard only

TRACK 45
keyboard plus
rhythm section

The left hand is playing a repeated root-5th and root-6th pattern on each chord, a staple of blues and blues-rock piano styles. The right-hand part is based around 3rd intervals from Mixolydian modes. For example, in the first measure, the intervals E–G, F–A, G–B♭, F–A and E–G from the C Mixolydian mode are used in the right hand over the C7 chord, on beats 1, 2, 3, 4 and the "and" of 4 respectively. These are combined with the root of C played with the thumb on most of the eighth note subdivisions, creating 3-part voicings (and sometimes 4-part when the C is doubled an octave higher). This pattern is then modified to fit the F Mixolydian mode over the F7 chord starting in measure 5, and so on. Half-step grace notes are also added to create the "bluesy" effect. The break in measure 10 uses descending 2nd inversion triads from the F Mixolydian mode, over the F7 chord. For more information on blues piano comping and phrasing, please check out my companion volume in this *Keyboard Style Series, Blues Piano: The Complete Guide with CD* (also published by Hal Leonard Corporation).

Philly Soul (70s)

Next, we'll look at some examples from the Philly Soul period, noted for its slick production and elaborate vocal harmonies, influenced by gospel and doo-wop. First, we have a straight eighths pattern in the style of "When Will I See You Again" by the Three Degrees. This was recorded with a Rhodes electric piano, and uses triad-over-root voicings with some arpeggios from measure 9, onwards. Note that the right-hand triads anticipate beat 3 by an eighth note, a common rhythmic figure across a range of pop, rock, and soul styles:

Comping pattern #10 – Style of "When Will I See You Again" by The Three Degrees

TRACK 46
keyboard only

TRACK 47
keyboard plus
rhythm section

The major chords are voiced simply by building major triads from the root. These are inverted over the 3rd (in measures 2, 6, 10 and 14) and over the 5th (in measures 4 and 12) to accommodate the descending left-hand bass line. In measures 3 and 11 we are building a D major triad from the 3rd of the Bm7 chords. In measures 7 and 15, we are building a G major triad from the 7th of the A11 chords. Note the "walkup" in 10th intervals connecting the A and D chords in measures 16–17, a common device in gospel-influenced R&B (as well as in gospel and country styles in general).

Next, we have a 6/4 pattern using eighth note triplets in the style of "If You Don't Know Me by Now" by Harold Melvin and the Blue Notes. As noted earlier, we can apply a swing eighths interpretation within 6/4 time, which will "swing" all eighth notes not written with triplet signs. This rhythmic feel actually originates from gospel music, which was a large influence on Philly soul. This example uses an acoustic piano with upper structure triad and four-part voicings, over a diatonic progression in the key of B major:

Comping pattern #11 – Style of "If You Don't Know Me by Now" by Harold Melvin and the Blue Notes

TRACK 48
keyboard only

TRACK 49
keyboard plus
rhythm section

Note that the main rhythmic "pulses" in this 6/4 style fall on beats 1 and 4 of the measure. The right hand is mostly playing upper structure voicings on beats 1 and 4, coinciding with the root in the left hand. The major chords (B and E) are voiced with major triads built from the root, the minor 7th chord (D♯m7) is voiced with a major triad built from the 3rd, and the dominant 11th (F♯11) is voiced by building a four-part minor 7th from the 5th. The right hand also leads into beat 4 with upper triad arpeggios (measures 1–4) and with alternating triads (IV–I in measure 5 and ♭VI–♭III in measure 6). Pentatonic scale fills are also used, within F♯ pentatonic, built from the 3rd of D♯m7 in measure 6, and within E pentatonic built from the root of E in measure 7 and from the 7th of F♯11 in measure 8. The left hand is also anticipating beats 3 and 6, effectively leading into the right hand figures on these downbeats. The gospel walk-up technique is again used to connect the F♯ and B major chords in measures 8–9.

Next, we have a 4/4 swing eighths pattern reminiscent of various gospel-style "shuffles" of the period. This uses acoustic piano, with a mix of alternating triad and Mixolydian triad voicings:

Comping pattern #12 - R&B/Gospel-style shuffle

TRACK 50
keyboard only

TRACK 51
keyboard plus
rhythm section

The left hand is playing a syncopated pattern using the root, 5th, and 6th of each chord, with eighth note "pickups" into beat 3 and some anticipations of beat 1. The right-hand part has similar rhythms, and uses ii–I alternating triads over the C major chords, and second inversion triads from the G Mixolydian mode over the G7 chords.

Funk (70s)

The next R&B style we will look at is funk, which offers many interesting options for keyboard players. This period saw the emergence of staccato-style funk comping on clavinet, as well as syncopated sixteenth-note grooves for piano and organ. First, we have a straight sixteenths pattern in the style of "Brick House" by the Commodores, which was recorded with a Rhodes electric piano. Both hands are mostly playing the same rhythms, emphasizing the anticipations:

Comping pattern #13 – Style of "Brick House" by The Commodores

TRACK 52
keyboard only

TRACK 53
keyboard plus
rhythm section

Here, the upper triads are simply built from the roots of the chord symbols, in first or second inversion. The top note of the right hand triads is doubled an octave lower in the left hand, creating an effective combined part.

Our next funk example is a swing sixteenths pattern in the style of "Shake" by the Gap Band. This also uses an electric piano sound, and mixes triad-over-root, suspended triad, and four-part-over-root voicings:

Comping pattern #14 – Style of "Shake" by The Gap Band

In measures 1–4 and 6–9, the right-hand voicings provide a continuous eighth-note pulse, except for the sixteenth-note anticipations of beat 1. In measures 5 and 10–14, the right hand anticipates beat 3 and plays on the 2nd sixteenth of beat 4, creating a more syncopated figure. The left hand starts out with whole-note roots, and then moves to a more driving feel with quarter notes played in octaves.

The E major chords are all voiced with a simple E major triad built from the root, and the Esus is a suspension of the E triad with the 4th (A) replacing the 3rd (G#). The dominant 11th (suspended dominant) chords are voiced either by building a four-part minor 7th from the 5th (as in the A11 chords) or by building a major triad from the 7th, with some octave doubling (as in the D11 and C11 chords). The dominant 7th chords are voiced either by building a diminished triad from the 3rd (as in the A7 chords) or with a 7–3 (7th and 3rd of the chord) voicing, with the root added (as in the B7 chord). The G major 9th chord is voiced by building a four-part minor 7th from the 3rd, with an inverted double 4th and a cluster shape added towards the end of the measure. The F major 7th chord is voiced by building a minor triad from the 3rd, and the B7sus chord is voiced with an inverted double 4th built from the root.

Our last example in this category is a straight sixteenths clavinet groove in the style of "Superstition" by Stevie Wonder. This type of staccato, syncopated comping is a signature sound in funk music, and is ideally suited to the clavinet due to its bright attack and percussive sound quality. This example uses 4th intervals from the G minor pentatonic scale, over different roots as follows:

Comping pattern #15 – Style of "Superstition" by Stevie Wonder

TRACK 56
keyboard only

TRACK 57
keyboard plus
rhythm section

Note that the 4th intervals from the G minor pentatonic scale (C–F, D–G, F–B♭, G–C) work over all of the chords in this progression. This voicing approach is based on the key of the tune (for example, using the G minor pentatonic scale in the key of G minor) rather than on a chord-by-chord basis.

The pattern is based on a rhythmic right hand figure which anticipates beat 4 by a sixteenth note. The left hand begins more sparsely in measures 1–8, playing the roots of the implied chords in octaves. In measure 9 the left hand starts using more of the "rhythmic spaces" between the notes in the right hand part, playing the root on beat 1 and different combinations of the 3rd, 5th, 7th and/or 9th afterwards. The priority here is the rhythmic interaction between the hands, and there are other left-hand note choices available (once the root is played on beat 1) within each chord—feel free to experiment! This overall approach is well suited to a wide range of R&B/funk comping styles which use the clavinet, from the 1970s, onwards.

Disco (70s)

Although disco tunes usually used simpler rhythms compared to some of the other R&B styles, the funk influence is still felt in the grooves and keyboard parts. A lot of the keyboard comping parts on disco tunes used synthesizer sounds (mostly analog), as well as piano (acoustic and electric). Our first disco pattern uses straight sixteenth rhythms and is in the style of "We Are Family" by Sister Sledge. The acoustic piano part is based on triad voicings, and adds fills in the upper register using octaves:

Comping pattern #16 — Style of "We Are Family" by Sister Sledge

TRACK 58
keyboard only

TRACK 59
keyboard plus
rhythm section

Here the triad-over-root voicings are all major triads simply built from the root, except for the G11 chords which are voiced by building a major triad from the 7th. In measures 1–8, the right hand lands on the "and" of 3 and "and" of 4, anticipating beat 4 and then beat 1 of the following measure. Starting at the end of measure 3, the top notes of the triads are doubled an octave below, adding to the energy and momentum.

The left hand starts out with simple root and 5th patterns, and then uses open triad arpeggios starting in measure 5 (normally root–5th–3rd on each chord, except for the root–7th–11th used on the G11). The right hand adds octave fills from measure 9, starting on beat 3, and leading into the triad anticipation on the "and" of 4, using notes from both the A major and A natural minor (or A Aeolian) scales. These gospel-influenced right-hand fills are useful across a range of pop, rock, and R&B styles. Finally, the ending phrase in measure 17 uses notes from the A pentatonic scale.

Our next disco example is a straight eighths pattern in the style of "Flashdance" by Irene Cara. This comping groove is recorded using an analog synth sound, which was very common for the period. It uses an effective mix of arpeggios, triad-over-root, and alternating triad voicings:

Comping pattern #17 – Style of "Flashdance" by Irene Cara

TRACK 60
keyboard only

TRACK 61
keyboard plus
rhythm section

The right-hand arpeggios in measure 1–6 are based on simple major and minor triads built from the roots of the chord symbols. Note the anticipation of beat 3 in all these measures, and the anticipation of beat 1 in measures 2 and 4. In measures 5 and 6, the right hand plays two notes from the upper triad on beat 1, which adds a little more energy. Then, starting in measure 7, we have some alternating triad voicings; I–V on Bb, bVII–I on G7, I–V on C, and II–I on F. Also, the Am7 and Dm7 chords are voiced by building a major triad from the 3rd, and the Gsus is voiced with an inverted double 4th and with a triad built from the 7th (upgrading it to a suspended dominant chord). On the C/E chords in measures 10 and 14 we are simply placing a C triad in the right hand over the 3rd of the C chord (E) in the left hand—these are still "C chords," but with the 3rd in the bass voice.

Our last disco example is a straight sixteenths pattern in the style of "Raining Men" by the Weather Girls. Although this example mostly uses eighth-note rhythms, there are some sixteenth-note anticipations of beat 4 in measures 2, 4, and 6 which are very important to the groove. Adding some sixteenth-note anticipations into an otherwise predominantly eighth-note feel is a useful technique, not only in disco, but in uptempo dance/pop styles in general. Again, the keyboard part was recorded using a characteristic analog synth pad:

Comping pattern #18 – Style of "Raining Men" by The Weather Girls

TRACK 62
keyboard only

TRACK 63
keyboard plus
rhythm section

In measures 1–6, the upper Fm, D♭, and E♭ triads are all placed over a "pedal point" (continuous bass note) of F. Otherwise, the voicings are mostly upper triads or suspensions built from the roots of the chord symbols, with variations such as resolutions within triads, and alternating triad voicings. The Csus–C movement in measures 7–8, 11, 15, and 19 is a "four-to-three" movement within the C triad. The E♭sus–E♭ movement in measures 10, 14, and 18 is a "four-to-three" movement within the E♭ triad, and in measure 20, a "four-to-three" movement is also used to embellish the Fm chord. The A♭/D♭ and D♭ chords in measures 21–22, and the A♭/E♭ and E♭ chords in measures 23–24, create V–I and IV–I (above the bass notes) alternating triad "pairs" respectively. The Cm/E♭ chords are simply C minor triads placed over the 3rd (E♭) in the left hand. Rhythmically speaking, note the emphasis on beat 2 at the start of the 4-measure phrases starting in measures 9, 13, 17, and 21, preceded by the left hand playing on beat 1 and the "& of 1" in octaves. In general, the left hand is playing the chord root on beat 1 (and also on beat 3 in many cases) followed by the root an octave higher on the upbeat, often leading into a triad voicing on beats 2 and/or 4 in the right hand (the "backbeats"). This rhythmic template is useful across a range of eighth-note pop, rock, and R&B styles.

R&B Ballad (80s)

Now we will change the mood a little to look at R&B ballad styles that emerged in the 1980s. This was a very smooth and polished sound in which keyboards played a vital role. Electric piano sounds (and in particular, the bell-like, "digital" piano sound of the Yamaha DX-7 synthesizer) are firmly associated with this style. Most R&B ballads use either eighth-note triplets or straight sixteenth rhythms, with characteristic anticipations. Our first R&B ballad pattern uses eighth-note triplet rhythms and is in the style of "Your Love Is King" by Sade. This is recorded with a Rhodes-style electric piano, and uses a mix of triad-over-root and four-part-over-root voicings:

Comping pattern #19 – Style of "Your Love Is King" by Sade

TRACK 64
keyboard only

TRACK 65
keyboard plus
rhythm section

Note that the overall feel of this example is "swing eighths," so all eighth notes which are not under triplet signs should be interpreted as quarter-eighth triplets. Generally, the right hand voicings land on beat 1, and then anticipate beat 3 by an eighth note. In measures 1–4, the left hand uses the same rhythm with simple root-5th voicings. From measure 5 onwards, the right-hand upper shapes are arpeggiated or "split" during beat 4, and the left hand plays "pickups" an eighth note ahead of the right hand (for example, playing the 5th of the chord on beat 2 leading into the right-hand voicing on the "and" of 2, and playing on the "and" of 3, leading into the right-hand voicing or arpeggio on beat 4). This left-hand rhythmic "pickup" function is a vital component of R&B piano styles. The major 7th and major 9th chords are all voiced with either minor triads or minor 7th chords built from the 3rd. The minor 7th chords are voiced with major triads built from the 3rd, and the suspended dominant chord is voiced with a major triad built from the 7th.

Next up, we have a straight sixteenth pattern in the style of "Greatest Love of All" by Whitney Houston, one of the quintessential R&B ballad examples of the period. Again, this uses rhythmic "pickups" and triad-over-root voicings, and is recorded with a "Yamaha DX"-type electric piano sound:

Comping pattern #20 – Style of "Greatest Love of All" by Whitney Houston

TRACK 66
keyboard only

TRACK 67
keyboard plus
rhythm section

It is important to understand the rhythmic interaction between the hands here, in order to successfully play this classic R&B ballad style. The right hand normally lands on all the downbeats, playing an upper structure voicing (complete or partial) on beats 1 and 3, and arpeggiating voicings during beat 2 (and sometimes beat 4). Meanwhile, the left hand plays the chord root on beats 1 and 3, and a rhythmic "pickup" leading into the backbeats (2 and 4) - either a sixteenth note ahead (as in measure 1, beat 2) or an eighth note ahead (as in measure 1, beat 4). The "pickup" note is normally the root, 5th, or 7th of the chord, and the left-hand part can be expanded to use open triad arpeggios (as in measures 9–10), range permitting. Use the sustain pedal as indicated, ensuring that you always release the pedal at the point of the chord change.

The minor 7th chords are all voiced with major triads built from the 3rd, and the suspended dominant chord (E11) is voiced with a major triad built from the 7th. Elsewhere, we simply have triads built from the root (as in the A, A+, D, and D+ chords) or a four-part literal spelling of the A7 chord. The E/D chords in measures 2 and 4 imply an inversion of an E7 dominant chord placed over the 7th in the bass, and the F#m/A and Bm/D chords are minor triads inverted over their 3rds in the bass. The A(add9) in measure 11 is created by adding the 9th (B) to the A major triad. Note that in measure 4, in the right hand, we have a fill using the D pentatonic scale during beat 2, and both "four-to-three" and "two-to-one" resolutions within the E major triad during beats 3 and 4 respectively.

Our last R&B ballad example is a straight sixteenth pattern in the style of "I Want the Night to Stay" by Luther Vandross. This sparser, more sophisticated groove uses double 4th and triad voicings, and is recorded with a synthesized electric piano sound:

Comping pattern #21 — Style of "I Want the Night to Stay" by Luther Vandross

TRACK 68
keyboard only

TRACK 69
keyboard plus
rhythm section

The right-hand part in measures 1–8 is based on the double 4th shape C–F–B♭, inverted in various ways, and placed over the chord roots as indicated. Using double 4ths over different chords in this way is common in contemporary jazz and new age styles, and is also heard in more harmonically advanced R&B ballads. In measures 9 and 10, a different double 4th (A♭–D♭–G♭, inverted and with the top note doubled) is used on the G♭(add9) chords, with the C–F–B♭ double 4th returning on the B♭(add9) chord in measure 12.

Otherwise, an A♭ triad is built from the 9th of the implied G♭ major chord in measures 9 and 10, and the minor 7th chords are voiced with major triads built from the 3rd in measure 11.

The rhythmic feel is very open in measures 1–8, with simple roots in the left hand and light sixteenth-note anticipations in the right hand double 4th figure. The energy builds from measure 9, with the left hand playing quarter note pedal points in octaves (and anticipating beat 4), and the right hand using a busier rhythmic figure, anticipating beats 2 and 3, and arpeggiating the upper structures during beat 4 in measures 9 and 10.

Dance/Pop (80s/90s)

Dance/pop followed the disco era and incorporated substantial rock and funk influences. Again, the keyboardist plays a vital role in this style, using piano, organ, clavinet, and/or synth as needed. Our first dance/pop example is a straight eighths pattern in the style of "How Will I Know" by Whitney Houston, an artist equally adept at hard-hitting dance tunes as well as sensitive ballads. This example was recorded with an analog synth sound, and uses triad-over-root, alternating triad, and suspended voicings:

**Comping pattern #22 – Style of "How Will I Know"
by Whitney Houston**

TRACK 70
keyboard only

TRACK 71
keyboard plus
rhythm section

Note the legato voicing style used in the right hand, with some notes tied over, between alternating triads. The left and right hands both "lock up" on the eighth note anticipations (for example, on the "and" of 4 in measure 1, the "and" of 2 in measure 2, and so on) which imparts some extra energy and momentum. The right hand uses alternating triads in measures 1, 3, 5, and 7; ♭VI–♭III on B♭m7 and ♭VII–♭III on A♭m7.

Otherwise, the C♭maj7 chords are voiced with a minor triad built from the 3rd, and the D♭11 chords are voiced with a major triad built from the 7th. The E♭sus chords are voiced by replacing the 3rd of an E♭m triad with the 4th, equivalent to an inverted double 4th shape (E♭–A♭–B♭). The left hand generally plays the roots of the chords on beats 1 and 3, or their anticipations.

Next, we have a straight eighths pattern in the style of "Cream" by Prince, a noted innovator in the dance/pop field, one who often uses unexpected textures or rhythms to positive effect. This example is recorded with an electric organ sound, and uses a mix of double 4ths, pentatonic 4th intervals, triads, and "bluesy" grace note phrases:

Comping pattern #23 – Style of "Cream" by Prince

TRACK 72
keyboard only

TRACK 73
keyboard plus
rhythm section

In measure 1, the right hand plays a double 4th built from the root of the B♭sus on beat 1, followed by a root-5th-root voicing on beat 2, and ending on a ♭3–3 resolution on the B♭7 chord during beat 4. In measure 2, the comping pattern uses 4th intervals from the E♭ minor pentatonic scale (A♭–D♭ and B♭–E♭) over the E♭7sus. Similar voicings and resolutions are used until measure 8, with the left hand playing the root on beat 1, and then playing the root and/or 5th on different upbeats, in the "rhythmic spaces" between the downbeats in the right hand.

In measure 9, the keyboard part changes to a steady eighth note comping using triads in the right hand. In measures 9–14, diminished triads are built from the 3rds of the B♭7 and F7 dominant chords (these triads are also found in the B♭ and F Mixolydian modes, respectively). The E♭ and B♭ chords are voiced simply with major triads built from the roots, and the phrase in the last half of measure 15 (over the Gm7 chord) is derived from the B♭ pentatonic scale.

Next up, we have a straight sixteenths pattern in the style of "Emotions" by Mariah Carey. This was recorded using acoustic piano, and utilizes a mix of triad-over-root, alternating triads, pentatonic riffs, and arpeggios:

Comping pattern #24 — Style of "Emotions" by Mariah Carey

TRACK 74
keyboard only

TRACK 75
keyboard plus
rhythm section

Note the two hands "locking together" in measures 1, 3, 5, 7, and 10 to create a classic dance/pop rhythmic groove: landing on beat 1, the "and" of 2, beat 3, the last 16th of beat 3, and the "and" of 4. We are building major triads from the 5th of the F major chords in measures 1, 3, 5, and 10 (as indicated by the C/F chord symbols), and a minor 7th from the 3rd of the Fmaj9 chord in measure 7. Elsewhere, the minor 7th chords are voiced by building major triads from the 3rd, and the (suspended) dominant 11th chords are voiced by building major triads from the 7th (with some octave doubling). The Dm7 is voiced with ♭III–♭VII alternating triads in measure 8, and the upper triad shapes are arpeggiated in measures 6 and 9. The staccato unison riff in measure 2 is derived from the A minor pentatonic scale.

Our last dance/pop example is a funkier groove in the style of "Precious" by Annie Lennox. This was recorded using a clavinet sound, and features the busier comping rhythms sometimes found in mid-tempo R&B/funk styles. The chord progression here is a twelve-bar "minor blues," starting with the I or tonic chord (Dm7) in measure 1, moving to the IV (Gm7) in measure 5, back to the I in measure 7, then to the V (A7) in measure 9, the IV in measure 10, and returning to the I chord in measure 11. There are many variations available on twelve-bar blues progressions—this particular one uses minor 7th chords from the I and IV, and a dominant 7th chord from the V. The right hand uses a mix of triad-over-root, alternating triad, pentatonic 4th interval, and 7–3 voicings, over a single-note left-hand part in the "rhythmic spaces" between the right hand shapes:

Comping pattern #25 – Style of "Precious" by Annie Lennox

TRACK 76
keyboard only

TRACK 77
keyboard plus
rhythm section

Rhythmically, the right hand plays an upper triad voicing on the "and" of 1, beat 2, the "and" of 2, and the last 16th of beat 2 (anticipating beat 3) of each measure. The left hand plays the chord root on beat 1 of each measure, and then a mixture of roots, 5ths, and 7ths in the rhythmic spaces between the right hand voicings. Harmonically, the right hand makes use of ♭III–♭VII alternating triads on all of the minor 7th chords, and a C♯ diminshed triad is built from the 3rd of the A7 chord in measure 9 (which is also available within the A Mixolydian mode). This measure also uses a 7–3 voicing on the A7 chord, and moves from the ♭3rd (C) to the 3rd (C♯) within this chord. Elsewhere, we see the use of pentatonic 4th intervals or fills from beat 3 onwards, in most measures, and the ending phrase in measure 12 uses 4th intervals from the D minor pentatonic scale.

Neo-Soul (90s/00s)

The neo-soul era began in the 1990s and is still going strong in this new millennium, combining hip-hop rhythms and production values with classic soul melodies and song forms. Vintage electric piano sounds (for example, Fender Rhodes) lend that authentic "retro" touch to many neo-soul recordings. Our first neo-soul example is a swing sixteenths pattern in the style of "All Day Thinkin'" by Babyface, one of the most popular artists in this genre. This example was recorded with a Rhodes-style electric piano sound, and uses a mix of triad and four-part upper structures, arpeggios, clusters, and pentatonic 4th intervals:

Comping pattern #26 — Style of "All Day Thinkin'"
by Babyface

TRACK 78
keyboard only

TRACK 79
keyboard plus
rhythm section

Rhythmically the right hand plays chord voicings on beat 1 of each measure, and on beat 3 in measures 1–3, 5–6 and 9. Also note the syncopated accent on the second 16th of beat 2, in these measures. The left hand plays the root of each chord on beats 1 and 3, and a rhythmic "pickup" or anticipation leading into beats 2 and 4 (the backbeats). Harmonically, on the F# and B minor 7th chords, we are building major triads from the 3rd. On the E minor 9th chords, we are building a major 7th four-part shape from the 3rd. We are also building minor 7th four-part shapes from the 3rd of the C major 9th chord and from the 5th of the A11 (suspended dominant) chord. The voicings on the G(add9) chord are based on a cluster (A–B–D), and the 4th interval fills in measures 7 and 8 are derived from the E minor pentatonic scale.

Next, we have a busier swing sixteenths pattern in the style of "Virtual Insanity" by Jamiroquai. This British band is noted for its innovative blend of jazz, funk, soul, and pop influences. This example was recorded with an acoustic piano sound, and predominantly uses four-part-over-root voicings:

Comping pattern #27 – Style of "Virtual Insanity" by Jamiroquai

TRACK 80
keyboard only

TRACK 81
keyboard plus
rhythm section

In this pattern, the left-hand roots are played on beats 1 and 3 of each measure, and the right hand voicing follows a sixteenth note later (for example, on the 2nd sixteenth of beats 1 and 3). The left hand also adds a "pickup" leading into the chord roots, a sixteenth note earlier (for example, on the last 16th of beats 2 and 4). The right-hand voicings are all based on four-part upper structures. The minor 9th chords are voiced by building major 7th chords from the 3rd, and the major 9th chords are voiced by building minor 7th chords from the 3rd. The dominant 9th chords are voiced by building minor 7th(♭5) shapes from the 3rd, and the B7sus and B7 chords in measures 4 and 8 are voiced simply by inverting basic 1–4–5–♭7 and 1–3–5–♭7 shapes, respectively. Starting in measure 4, we also arpeggiate the four-part upper structures during beats 2 and/or 4, adding to the energy level.

Next up, we have a more mellow, straight sixteenths pattern in the style of "A Woman's Worth" by Alicia Keys, whose piano stylings are at the forefront of today's neo-soul. This example was recorded with a Rhodes-style electric piano sound and uses triad-over-root, alternating triad, and four-part-over-root voicings, together with a distinctive left hand bass line:

Comping pattern #28 – Style of "A Woman's Worth" by Alicia Keys

TRACK 82
keyboard only

TRACK 83
keyboard plus
rhythm section

The bass line starts on the root of each chord and moves to the 5th, 7th (6th on the Gmaj9 chord), and then back to the root. Against this, the right hand upper shapes only use whole note rhythms in measures 1–4, before adding more subdivisions ("and" of 3, 2nd sixteenth of beat 4) from measure 5. The minor 7th chords are all voiced with major triads built from the 3rd, and with ♭III–♭VII alternating triads in measures 5 and 7. There is a "2 to 1" resolution inside the D triad built from the 3rd of the Bm7 chord during beat 4 of measure 6. The D11 (suspended dominant) chords are voiced with major triads built from the 7th, and the G major 9th chords are voiced with a minor 7th built from the 3rd.

Our final neo-soul example is a straight sixteenths pattern in the style of "She's All I Got" by Jimmy Cozier. This was recorded with an electric piano sound, and uses some double 4th voicings, along with the upper triads and four-part shapes to create a more sophisticated impression:

Comping Pattern #29 — Style of "She's All I Got" by Jimmy Cozier

TRACK 84
keyboard only

TRACK 85
keyboard plus
rhythm section

Here the minor 7th chords are all voiced with major triads built from the 3rd. The Bmaj9 chord is voiced with a minor 7th shape built from the 3rd, and the D♭11 and G♭11 chords are voiced with major triads built from the 7th (with octave doubling on the D♭11). Elsewhere on the inverted major chords, we are using double 4th shapes, for example, in measure 2, we have the C–F–B double 4th built from the 9th of the B♭ chord, inverted over the 3rd in the left hand. Both hands are playing the chord voicing on beat 1 of each measure, with frequent right hand accents on the "and" of 3 and the 2nd sixteenth of beat 4. The ending figure in measure 18 uses fourth intervals from the E♭ minor pentatonic scale.

Chapter 5
STYLE FILE

In this chapter we have seven tunes written in different R&B styles. The keyboard parts for these tunes mainly focus on the "comping" or chordal accompaniment patterns typically required of the R&B keyboardist. These examples use a mix of upper structure voicings in the right hand, over single-note or arpeggiated patterns in the left hand. These voicings were defined back in Chapter 3, and are used in the comping examples throughout Chapter 4. In some tunes, the keyboard plays an improvised solo in the right hand, in which case the left hand takes over the upper structure voicings, around the middle C area.

These tunes use a variety of different keyboard instruments: acoustic piano, electric piano, organ, clavinet, or synthesizer, depending on the R&B style required. For some tunes, the recorded tracks include a melody instrument, which is then accompanied by the keyboard part.

We will also analyze the "form" of each tune. This involves the labeling of the different sections (for example, Intro, A section or Verse, B section or Chorus, C Section or Bridge, Solo, Coda etc.). In this chapter, we will use the labels "A," "B," and "C" (also known as **rehearsal letters**) as we are focusing on the instrumental parts. However, as R&B is a vocal-oriented style, be aware that labels such as **verse**, **chorus**, and **bridge** are also commonly used.

The Intro section (if present) normally establishes the rhythmic groove and style of the tune. Next, the "A section" occurs when the first melody or theme is introduced, and will often use a chord progression similar to the Intro. From a vocal standpoint, this is normally the "Verse," which tells the lyrical story of the song. If the tune then builds into a different melody section or "hook," the label "B section" can be used (which for vocal tunes is normally the "Chorus"). If the tune transitions into another, different section, the label "C section" can be used (which for vocal tunes might be the "Bridge," as a variation after one or more Choruses). The "Solo section" is where an improvised instrumental solo occurs, normally over the chord progression from an earlier section of the tune (for example "A" or "B"). Finally, there may be a separate Coda, which is the ending section.

These tunes were all recorded with a band (bass, drums, and comping/melody instruments) as well as keyboard. On the CD tracks, the band (minus the keyboard) is on the left channel, and the keyboard is on the right channel. To play along with the band on these tunes, just turn down the right channel. Slow as well as full speed tracks are provided on the CD for each song, except for tune #7, which is already at a slow ballad tempo.

1. Soul Genius

The first tune is written in the style of "One Mint Julep" by Ray Charles. This is a mid-tempo, straight eighths groove in the key of E♭, recorded with an electric organ sound. The chord progression is based on a 12-bar blues form, with some jazz-tinged variations. These include the ♭VI–V in measures 9–10, and the I–VI–ii–V turnaround in measures 11–12. The first A section (measures 1–12) introduces the melody, derived from the E♭ blues scale, played in octave unison between the hands. Improvised fills are inserted in measures 4, 8, and over the turnaround in measures 11–12. The second A section (measures 13–24) repeats the same melody, but adds busier fills in the spaces. The B section (measures 25–32) uses a descending series of dominant 13th voicings and rhythmic syncopations leading into the Solo section (measures 33-40), which alternates between dominant chords built from the I and IV. The organ solo over this section is derived from the E♭ blues scale, and the left hand adds some 7–3 voicings in the rhythmic spaces. Finally, the last A section (measures 41–52) restates the main melody, adding new and more elaborate fills in the spaces.

Make sure the unison riffs in the A sections, and the syncopated voicings in the B section are cleanly articulated with both hands. Once you have the E♭ blues scale under your fingers, you can work on your own fills in the A sections, as well as your own blues improvisation in the Solo section!

TRACK 86 slow   TRACK 87 full speed

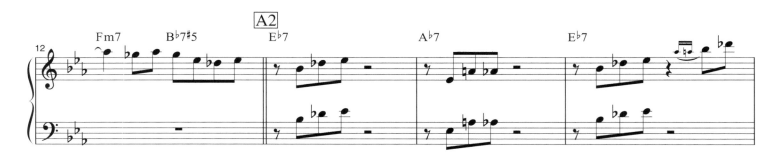

2. Whenever I'm with You

Next up is a tune written in the style of "Heat Wave" by Martha Reeves and the Vandellas. This has an up-tempo swing eighths feel, typical of the pop-oriented soul music produced by Motown in the 1960s. In this example, the keyboard comping is handled by the acoustic piano. The Intro (measures 1–4) sets up the rhythmic feel using fourth intervals from the E♭ pentatonic scale in a repeated eighth-note pattern. Then in the first A section (measures 5–18), triad-over-root voicings are used, with both hands anticipating beat 3 (except for measures 11–12, which use a similar pattern to the Intro). Measures 19–22 repeat the Intro, followed by the second A section (measures 23–36) which arpeggiates the upper triads towards the end of each measure. Here, an organ melody is added above the piano comping, and a baritone sax riff reinforces the bass line. Finally, the Coda section (measures 37–41) ends the tune with an extended repeat of the Intro.

Make sure the right hand fourth intervals in the Intro and Coda sections alternate evenly with the single notes played on the upbeats—practice this at a slower tempo first if necessary. Also ensure you're "in the pocket" on the anticipations of beat 3 in the A sections, as this is important to the style.

TRACK 88
slow

TRACK 89
full speed

3. Funk Jam

Our next example is a straight sixteenths groove in the style of "Outa Space" by Billy Preston, and features the syncopated funk comping style associated with Preston and other keyboard greats such as George Duke, Stevie Wonder, and Max Middleton. This example was recorded on clavinet, an instrument popularized by funk recordings from the 70s onwards. During the Intro (measures 1–4), the clavinet figure is derived from the E blues scale, and an organ pad is added. Then in the first A section (measures 5–12), the main clavinet comping groove kicks in, using fourth intervals from the E minor pentatonic scale in the right hand, interspersed with single notes in the left hand. In the second A section (measures 13–20), a synth melody is added, and the comping figure gets busier, with more sixteenth-note subdivisions. In the B section (measures 21–28), the comping uses Mixolydian triads over the dominant chords: for example, over the C7 chord in measure 21, the upper triads Edim (implied by the E♭–E resolution), F, and Gm are all derived from the C Mixolydian mode. During the B section, a string melody is also added. The C section (measures 29–36) starts out as a "breakdown," with a sparser feel and more space in the clavinet figure, before adding a synth melody in measure 33. Then the D section (measures 37–44) blends the start of the Intro with the dominant chords from the B section, adding an organ pad and string melody. Finally, the Coda (measures 45–48) is a variation on the Intro, using the rhythm section feel from the A section.

These clavinet comping rhythms can be challenging for the novice keyboardist! Practise using the slower tempo first, as needed, and also isolate the right-hand part first, before adding the left-hand part in the "rhythmic spaces." As your confidence increases, try your own variations on the comping pattern. For example, use different fourth intervals from the E minor pentatonic scale in the A sections. Have fun, and stay in the groove!

TRACK 90
slow

TRACK 91
full speed

4. Inside Out

The next example is in the style of the tune "Upside Down" by Diana Ross, a disco classic with considerable funk and soul influences. This is a mid-tempo, straight sixteenths groove, recorded using an acoustic piano sound. The piano comping mainly uses triad-over-root voicings, with some octave doubling and added 9ths. In the Intro (measures 1–8), a resonant synth clav is added behind the piano voicings. Then in the first A section (measures 9–16), the main groove kicks in, with the piano adding some pentatonic fourth intervals to the triad-over-root voicings. A string synth is added to increase the energy level in measure 13. In the first B section (measures 17–24), a synth melody and an organ pad are both added, over a sparser piano comping pattern using triad and four-part voicings. The C section (measures 25–36) is a variation on the A section, with space added for piano fills in every other measure. These fills use a mix of blues and pentatonic scales and resolutions within upper triads. The second B section (measures 37–44) features a piano solo derived from the A blues scale, over triad and four-part voicings, now played by the left hand. Finally, the last A section (measures 45–54) is similar to the first, now with an organ pad and two extra measures added to the form to create a "tag" ending.

Ensure that the sixteenth note "upbeats" are articulated clearly in the piano part, and make sure the piano solo in the second B section projects over the left hand voicings. When you are comfortable with the written part, experiment with your own piano fills in the C section, and your own piano solo over the second B section!

TRACK 92
slow

TRACK 93
full speed

Intro
Piano – Straight 16ths

5. It'll Always Be This Way

Next up is a tune written in the style of "Sweet Love" by Anita Baker. This has a slow, straight eighths feel, with some occasional sixteenth-note subdivisions. The example was recorded with a "Yamaha DX"-style electric piano, which was widely used on R&B ballads in the 80s. The piano part is primarily based on four-part-over-root voicings, with some upper triads and arpeggios. The Intro (measures 1–8) adds some left-hand open triad arpeggios below the right-hand, four-part upper structures. In the first A section (measures 9–16), the piano part uses triad-over-root voicings, with some 5th and 6th intervals derived from these upper triads: for example, in measure 9, the E–B and G#–E intervals are both derived from inversions of the upper E major triad. Meanwhile, the left hand continues with open triad arpeggio patterns, and a string synth pad is added. In the first B section (measures 17–24), the synth melody is accompanied by right hand, four-part upper structures on all the eighth note subdivisions, emphasizing beat 1, the "and" of 2, and beat 4. The piano takes a solo during the second A section (measures 25–36), using pentatonic scale phrases over four-part upper structures being played by the left hand. A string pad is added in measure 29 to help build this section. The second B section (measures 37–48) is based on the first, but with busier chord rhythms and anticipations, with strings again being added in measure 45. Finally, the Coda (measures 49–53) is a variation on the Intro, with different arpeggios of the four-part upper structures during beat 4 of each measure.

Make sure the eighth-note upper structure patterns are clearly articulated in the B sections, and watch out for the extra chord changes added in the second B section. You should use the sustain pedal for the duration of each chord throughout the tune, except during the B sections, where the pedal detracts from the steady eighth-note pulse of the right hand voicings.

TRACK 94
slow

TRACK 95
full speed

74

6. Pump It Up

Our next example is written in the style of "Thriller" by Michael Jackson, one of the best-known examples of 80s R&B dance/pop. The keyboard part was recorded using an analog synth pad sound, which is very typical of the period. Although there are a lot of quarter and eighth notes in the keyboard part, there are also some important sixteenth note anticipations in both hands, which are sufficient to impart a "sixteenth note feel." In other words, I would consider this to be a straight sixteenths groove overall. In the Intro (measures 1–8), the synth plays triad-over-root voicings and suspensions, mostly using quarter-note rhythms, but with some sixteenth-note anticipations. In the first A section (measures 9–22), the left hand plays a repeated bass figure (or "ostinato") derived from the A minor pentatonic scale, under the right-hand triad voicings. This is all being used to accompany a synth melody. The B section (measures 23–29) functions as a rhythmic "breakdown," with the synth using alternating triad and cluster voicings over a descending bass line. The second A section (measures 30–33) is truncated to four measures in order to lead into the Intro repeat (measures 34–41), which is similar to the first Intro, but now with the "backbeat" added on the drums. Finally, the last A section (measures 42–50) is a variation on the first, with different chords leading to the ending riff derived from the A minor pentatonic scale.

Concentrate on the sixteenth-note subdivisions and anticipations when they occur (for example, the last sixteenth note in measure 9, anticipating beat 1 of the next measure). These can sometimes be lost in a groove which mostly uses quarter notes and eighth notes. Also make sure the left-hand synth part "locks up" with the bass on the recording, particularly on the repeated riff during the A sections.

TRACK 96
slow

TRACK 97
full speed

7. Urban Legend

Our last tune is a slow, straight sixteenths example in the style of "Anytime" by Brian McKnight, a well-known artist in today's neo-soul scene. This was recorded with an acoustic piano sound, and uses some more sophisticated voicing devices such as double 4ths and clusters. These sounds are common in contemporary jazz and new age/jazz styles, and are also used in the more jazz-influenced R&B styles. The Intro (measures 1–4) uses arpeggiated clusters in the right hand, over open triad arpeggio patterns in the left hand. In the first A section (measures 5–10), the synth melody enters, supported by double 4ths, resolutions within triads, and "add9" voicings in the right-hand piano part. The left hand now adds some root-7th voicings (a jazz staple) as well as open triad arpeggios. The synth melody continues into the first B section (measures 11–14), this time accompanied with clusters and 6th intervals in the piano part. The Intro repeat (measures 15–17) is truncated to 3 measures to lead into the second A section (measures 18–23), basically the same as the first A section, but with some variations in the chords. The second B section (measures 24–27) is a repeat of the first, leading into the last A section (measures 28–35), which adds some extra measures to create a "tag" ending.

Practice the left-hand open triad patterns separately as needed, before adding the right-hand part. Make sure to use the sustain pedal for the duration of each chord, and try to "lock up" with the synth melody during the A and B sections, as the piano is doubling this melody with the top note of the right-hand part. Have fun!

TRACK 98
full speed

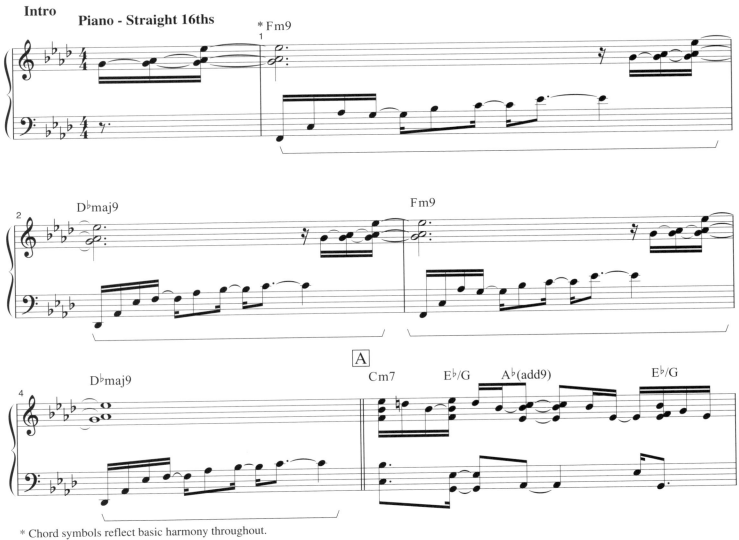

* Chord symbols reflect basic harmony throughout.

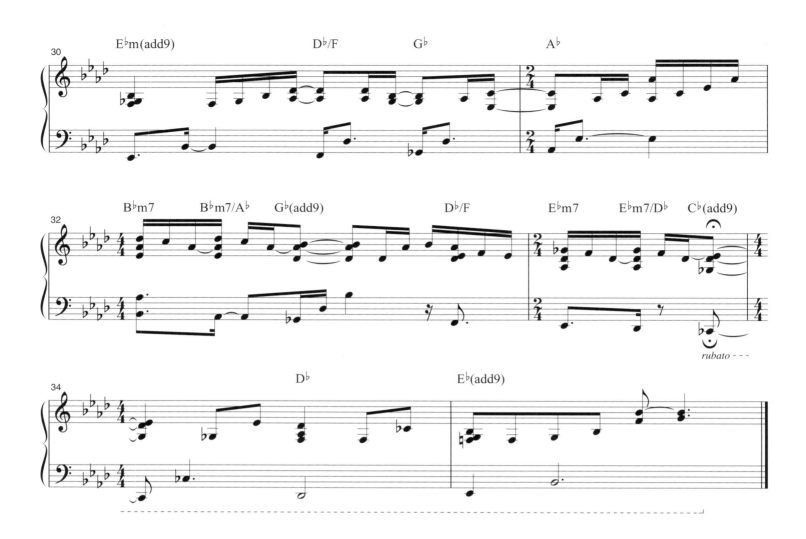

KEYBOARD STYLE SERIES

THE COMPLETE GUIDE WITH CD!

These book/CD packs provide focused lessons that contain valuable how-to insight, essential playing tips, and beneficial information for all players. From comping to soloing, comprehensive treatment is given to each subject. The companion CD features many of the examples in the book performed either solo or with a full band.

BEBOP JAZZ PIANO

by John Valerio

This book provides detailed information for bebop and jazz keyboardists on: chords and voicings, harmony and chord progressions, scales and tonality, common melodic figures and patterns, comping, characteristic tunes, the styles of Bud Powell and Thelonious Monk, and more. Includes 5 combo performances at the end of the book.
00290535 Book/CD Pack.....................................$17.95

BLUES PIANO

by Mark Harrison

With this book/CD pack, you'll learn the theory, the tools, and even the tricks that the pros use to play the blues. You also get seven complete tunes to jam with on the CD. Covers: scales and chords; left-hand patterns; walking bass; endings and turnarounds; right-hand techniques; how to solo with blues scales; crossover licks; and more.
00311007 Book/CD Pack.....................................$16.95

COUNTRY PIANO

by Mark Harrison

Learn the theory, the tools, and the tricks used by the pros to get that authentic country sound. This book/CD pack covers: scales and chords, walkup and walkdown patterns, comping in traditional and modern country, Nashville "fretted piano" techniques and more. At the end, you'll get to jam along with seven complete tunes.
00311052 Book/CD Pack.....................................$17.95

POST-BOP JAZZ PIANO

by John Valerio

This book/CD pack will teach you the basic skills needed to play post-bop jazz piano. Learn the theory, the tools, and the tricks used by the pros to play in the style of Bill Evans, Thelonious Monk, Herbie Hancock, McCoy Tyner, Chick Corea and others. Topics covered include: chord voicings, scales and tonality, modality, and more.
00311005 Book/CD Pack.....................................$17.95

R&B KEYBOARD

by Mark Harrison

From soul to funk to disco to pop, you'll learn the theory, the tools, and the tricks used by the pros with this book/CD pack. Topics covered include: scales and chords, harmony and voicings, progressions and comping, rhythmic concepts, characteristic stylings, the development of R&B, and more! Includes seven songs.
00310881 Book/CD Pack.....................................$17.95

ROCK KEYBOARD

by Scott Miller

Learn to comp or solo in any of your favorite rock styles. Listen to the CD to hear your parts fit in with the total groove of the band. Includes 99 tracks! Covers: classic rock, pop/rock, blues rock, Southern rock, hard rock, progressive rock, alternative rock and heavy metal.
00310823 Book/CD Pack.....................................$16.95

ROCK 'N' ROLL PIANO

by Andy Vinter

Take your place alongside Fats Domino, Jerry Lee Lewis, Little Richard, and other legendary players of the '50s and '60s! This book/CD pack covers: left-hand patterns; basic rock 'n' roll progressions; right-hand techniques; straight eighths vs. swing eighths; glisses, crushed notes, rolls, note clusters and more. Includes six complete tunes.
00310912 Book/CD Pack.....................................$16.95

SMOOTH JAZZ PIANO

by Mark Harrison

Learn the skills you need to play smooth jazz piano – the theory, the tools, and the tricks used by the pros. Topics covered include: scales and chords; harmony and voicings; progressions and comping; rhythmic concepts; melodies and soloing; characteristic stylings; discussions on jazz evolution.
00311095 Book/CD Pack.....................................$17.95

STRIDE & SWING PIANO

by John Valerio

Learn the styles of the stride and swing piano masters, such as Scott Joplin, Jimmy Yancey, Pete Johnson, Jelly Roll Morton, James P. Johnson, Fats Waller, Teddy Wilson, and Art Tatum. This book/CD pack covers classic ragtime, early blues and boogie woogie, New Orleans jazz and more. Includes 14 songs.
00310882 Book/CD Pack.....................................$17.95

FOR MORE INFORMATION, SEE YOUR LOCAL MUSIC DEALER, OR WRITE TO:

HAL•LEONARD®
CORPORATION
7777 W. BLUEMOUND RD. P.O. BOX 13819 MILWAUKEE, WI 53213

Visit Hal Leonard online at
www.halleonard.com

KEYBOARD *signature licks*

These exceptional book/CD packs teach keyboardists the techniques and styles used by popular artists from yesterday and today. Each folio breaks down the trademark riffs and licks used by these great performers.

BEST OF BEBOP PIANO

by Gene Rizzo

16 bebop piano transcriptions: April in Paris • Between the Devil and the Deep Blue Sea • I Don't Stand a Ghost of a Chance • If I Were a Bell • Lullaby of Birdland • On a Clear Day (You Can See Forever) • Satin Doll • Thou Swell • and more.
00695734..$19.95

CONTEMPORARY CHRISTIAN

by Todd Lowry

Learn the trademark keyboard styles and techniques of today's top contemporary Christian artists. 12 songs, including: Fool for You (Nichole Nordeman) • The Great Divide (Point of Grace) • His Strength Is Perfect (Steven Curtis Chapman) • How Beautiful (Twila Paris) • If I Stand (Rich Mullins) • Know You in the Now (Michael Card) • and more.
00695753..$19.95

BILL EVANS

by Brent Edstrom

12 songs from pianist Bill Evans, including: Five • One for Helen • The Opener • Peace Piece • Peri's Scope • Quiet Now • Re: Person I Knew • Time Remembered • Turn Out the Stars • Very Early • Waltz for Debby • 34 Skidoo.
00695714..$22.95

BEN FOLDS FIVE

by Todd Lowry

16 songs from four Ben Folds Five albums: Alice Childress • Battle of Who Could Care Less • Boxing • Brick • Don't Change Your Plans • Evaporated • Kate • The Last Polka • Lullabye • Magic • Narcolepsy • Philosophy • Song for the Dumped • Underground.
00695578..$22.95

BILLY JOEL CLASSICS: 1974-1980

by Robbie Gennet

15 popular hits from the '70s by Billy Joel: Big Shot • Captain Jack • Don't Ask Me Why • The Entertainer • Honesty • Just the Way You Are • Movin' Out (Anthony's Song) • My Life • New York State of Mind • Piano Man • Root Beer Rag • Say Goodbye to Hollywood • Scenes from an Italian Restaurant • She's Always a Woman • The Stranger.
00695581..$22.95

BILLY JOEL HITS: 1981-1993

by Todd Lowry

15 more hits from Billy Joel in the '80s and '90s: All About Soul • Allentown • And So It Goes • Baby Grand • I Go to Extremes • Leningrad • Lullabye (Goodnight, My Angel) • Modern Woman • Pressure • The River of Dreams • She's Got a Way • Tell Her About It • This Is the Time • Uptown Girl • You're Only Human (Second Wind).
00695582..$22.95

ELTON JOHN CLASSIC HITS

by Todd Lowry

10 of Elton's best are presented in this book/CD pack: Blue Eyes • Chloe • Don't Go Breaking My Heart • Don't Let the Sun Go Down on Me • Ego • I Guess That's Why They Call It the Blues • Little Jeannie • Sad Songs (Say So Much) • Someone Saved My Life Tonight • Sorry Seems to Be the Hardest Word.
00695688..$22.95

LENNON & MCCARTNEY HITS

by Todd Lowry

Features 15 hits from A-L for keyboard by the legendary songwriting team of John Lennon and Paul McCartney. Songs include: All You Need Is Love • Back in the U.S.S.R. • The Ballad of John and Yoko • Because • Birthday • Come Together • A Day in the Life • Don't Let Me Down • Drive My Car • Get Back • Good Day Sunshine • Hello, Goodbye • Hey Jude • In My Life • Lady Madonna.
00695650..$22.95

LENNON & MCCARTNEY FAVORITES

by Todd Lowry

16 more hits (L-Z) from The Beatles: Let It Be • The Long and Winding Road • Lucy in the Sky with Diamonds • Martha My Dear • Ob-La-Di, Ob-La-Da • Oh! Darling • Penny Lane • Revolution 9 • Rocky Raccoon • She's a Woman • Strawberry Fields Forever • We Can Work It Out • With a Little Help from My Friends • The Word • You're Going to Lose That Girl • Your Mother Should Know.
00695651..$22.95

BEST OF ROCK

by Todd Lowry

12 songs are analyzed: Bloody Well Right (Supertramp) • Cold as Ice (Foreigner) • Don't Do Me Like That (Tom Petty & The Heartbreakers) • Don't Let the Sun Go Down on Me (Elton John) • I'd Do Anything for Love (Meat Loaf) • Killer Queen (Queen) • Lady Madonna (The Beatles) • Light My Fire (The Doors) • Piano Man (Billy Joel) • Point of No Return (Kansas) • Separate Ways (Journey) • Werewolves of London (Warren Zevon).
00695751..$19.95

BEST OF ROCK 'N' ROLL PIANO

by David Bennett Cohen

12 of the best hits for piano are presented in this pack. Songs include: At the Hop • Blueberry Hill • Brown-Eyed Handsome Man • Charlie Brown • Great Balls of Fire • Jailhouse Rock • Lucille • Rock and Roll Is Here to Stay • Runaway • Tutti Frutti • Yakety Yak • You Never Can Tell.
00695627..$19.95

BEST OF STEVIE WONDER

by Todd Lowry

This book/CD pack includes musical examples, lessons, biographical notes, and more for 14 of Stevie Wonder's best songs. Features: I Just Called to Say I Love You • My Cherie Amour • Part Time Lover • Sir Duke • Superstition • You Are the Sunshine of My Life • and more.
00695605..$22.95

Prices, contents and availability subject to change without notice.

0304

NOTE-FOR-NOTE KEYBOARD TRANSCRIPTIONS

These outstanding collections feature note-for-note transcriptions from the artists who made the songs famous.
No matter what style you play, these books are perfect for performers or students who want to play just like their keyboard idols.

ACOUSTIC PIANO BALLADS

16 acoustic piano favorites: Angel • Candle in the Wind • Don't Let the Sun Go Down on Me • Endless Love • Imagine • It's Too Late • Let It Be • Mandy • Ribbon in the Sky • Sailing • She's Got a Way • So Far Away • Tapestry • You Never Give Me Your Money • You've Got a Friend • Your Song.

00690351 / $19.95

ELTON JOHN

18 of Elton John's best songs: Bennie and the Jets • Candle in the Wind • Crocodile Rock • Daniel • Don't Let the Sun Go Down on Me • Goodbye Yellow Brick Road • I Guess That's Why They Call It the Blues • Little Jeannie • Rocket Man • Your Song and more!

00694829 / $19.95

THE BEATLES KEYBOARD BOOK

23 Beatles favorites, including: All You Need Is Love • Back in the U.S.S.R. • Come Together • Get Back • Good Day Sunshine • Hey Jude • Lady Madonna • Let It Be • Lucy in the Sky with Diamonds • Ob-La-Di, Ob-La-Da • Oh! Darling • Penny Lane • Revolution • We Can Work It Out • With a Little Help from My Friends • and more.

00694827 / $19.95

THE CAROLE KING KEYBOARD BOOK

16 of King's greatest songs: Beautiful • Been to Canaan • Home Again • I Feel the Earth Move • It's Too Late • Jazzman • (You Make Me Feel) Like a Natural Woman • Nightingale • Smackwater Jack • So Far Away • Sweet Seasons • Tapestry • Way Over Yonder • Where You Lead • Will You Love Me Tomorrow • You've Got a Friend.

00690554 / $19.95

CLASSIC ROCK

35 all-time rock classics: Beth • Bloody Well Right • Changes • Cold as Ice • Come Sail Away • Don't Do Me Like That • Hard to Handle • Heaven • Killer Queen • King of Pain • Layla • Light My Fire • Oye Como Va • Piano Man • Takin' Care of Business • Werewolves of London • and more.

00310940 / $24.95

POP/ROCK

35 songs, including: Africa • Against All Odds • Axel F • Centerfold • Chariots of Fire • Cherish • Don't Let the Sun Go Down on Me • Drops of Jupiter (Tell Me) • Faithfully • It's Too Late • Just the Way You Are • Let It Be • Mandy • Sailing • Sweet Dreams Are Made of This • Walking in Memphis • and more.

00310939 / $24.95

JAZZ

24 favorites from Bill Evans, Thelonious Monk, Oscar Peterson, Bud Powell, and Art Tatum and more. Includes: Ain't Misbehavin' • April in Paris • Autumn in New York • Body and Soul • Freddie Freeloader • Giant Steps • My Funny Valentine • Satin Doll • Song for My Father • Stella by Starlight • and more.

00310941 / $22.95

R&B

35 R&B classics: Baby Love • Boogie on Reggae Woman • Easy • Endless Love • Fallin' • Green Onions • Higher Ground • I'll Be There • Just Once • Money (That's What I Want) • On the Wings of Love • Ribbon in the Sky • This Masquerade • Three Times a Lady • and more.

00310942 / $24.95

THE BILLY JOEL KEYBOARD BOOK

16 mega-hits from the Piano Man himself: Allentown • And So It Goes • Honesty • Just the Way You Are • Movin' Out • My Life • New York State of Mind • Piano Man • Pressure • She's Got a Way • Tell Her About It • and more.

00694828 / $22.95

STEVIE WONDER

14 of Stevie's most popular songs: Boogie on Reggae Woman • Hey Love • Higher Ground • I Wish • Isn't She Lovely • Lately • Living for the City • Overjoyed • Ribbon in the Sky • Send One Your Love • Superstition • That Girl • You Are the Sunshine of My Life • You Haven't Done Nothin'.

00306698 / $19.95

Prices, contents and availability subject to change without notice.

FOR MORE INFORMATION, SEE YOUR LOCAL MUSIC DEALER,
OR WRITE TO:

HAL•LEONARD®
CORPORATION
7777 W. BLUEMOUND RD. P.O. BOX 13819 MILWAUKEE, WI 53213

Visit Hal Leonard online at **www.halleonard.com**